The Wanderer: Daniel Boone's Kentucke

by

Eugene Goss

Authored, printed, and manufactured in the U.S.A. Typeset by Skybridge Press Corp. Cover design and photo by John Fritz. Cover photo of the historic Patterson Cabin, used with permission (see Acknowledgments) is not intended to express nor imply endorsement of the content of this book.

Subject Author Intelligence Data (SAID)
Analogue Abstract

Goss, Eugene
The Wanderer: Daniel Boone's Kentucke
    Second Edition
6 x 9 x 0.57 in.; 252 pp.; bibliography; illustrated,
    large print (14 point).
ISBN-13: 978-1505586466
ISBN-10: 1505586461
I. Goss, Eugene.; II. Title;
    A. Daniel Boone, biography;
    B. Kentucky, History of;
    C. Rebecca Bryan Boone;
    D. Transylvania Company;
    E. Richard Henderson;
    F. Nonfiction, historical.

Dedication

For

Mark David and Becky Goss

and

My granddaughters,
Elizabeth and Sarah

and

Cy Layson, my old hunting buddy

———————

The Wanderer

From a majestic forest,
there came a thousand songs,
all in perfect harmony,
giving way from time to time
to the sounds of that rude interloper.

Fearless herds of bison wandered aimlessly
from place to place without seeming purpose.

Furry animals scampered to their holes,
hiding themselves from the strange intruder.

The resplendent forest burst with the many colors
of spring — the greens, reds, and other vibrant
colors — as the season called them out.

He witnessed all the sights and sounds of the
forest — untouched, serene, and complete.

Then did the dreamer first feel his soul give over
to the splendor and beauty of this place.

He had found the perfect Eden.

He will have it for his own.

———————

Acknowledgments

Of the people who helped me with this book, I thank Neal O. Hammon of Shelbyville, Kentucky, and Ted Franklin Belue of Murray, Kentucky, renown scholars of early Kentucky history, who took time out of their busy lives to read my manuscript and make substantive recommendations regarding its content. I also thank Neal O. Hammon for furnishing very helpful maps of Kentucky from his collection. I especially thank Brenda Cassim, my secretary for 43 years, and Brenda Kelly, a patient reader, who helped keep this project going.

Cover design and photo by John Fritz. Cover photo depicting the historic Patterson Cabin, maintained by Transylvania University, Lexington, Ky., is used with permission; and, is not intended to express nor imply endorsement of the content of this book. A Kentucky Historical Society marker states that the cabin was built before 1780. Some historians think the cabin, which has been restored twice, is representative of frontier homes of the era of Daniel Boone (1734-1820).

Table of Contents

Introduction

"... Here, where the hand of violence shed the blood of the innocent; where the horrid yells of savages, and the groans of the distressed, sounded in our ears, we now hear the praises and adoration of our Creator; where wretched wigwams stood, the miserable abodes of savages, we behold the foundations of cities laid, that, in all probability, will rival the glory of the greatest upon the earth. And we view Kentucke situated on the fertile banks of the great Ohio, rising from obscurity to shine with splendor, equal of any other of the stars of the American hemisphere." – Colonel Daniel Boone

Whether it was Joshua beating on the gates of Jericho, Alexander loosening his forces on Persia, or Napoleon on a mission of world conquest, the prize was nearly always the same: it's land!

During the middle of the Eighteenth Century, fierce competition erupted on several fronts in North America; fertile new lands were found ready for settlement and exploitation, as was much of North America west of the Alleghenies. Efforts by competing powers and people to own and ex-

exploit those lands sparked savage acts of cruelty and depravity. However, there were also many acts of bravery by rugged and fearless men, like Daniel Boone, who faced countless challenges in a lifetime of adventure in the wilderness of Kentucky.

During that same time, the lands on the frontier east of the Mississippi were almost a constant source of conflict. Great Britain and France fought a long war over the ownership of unsettled wilderness lands, and also over profits from the fur trade. That war ended in a truce, expelling the French from North America.

Soon after, squatters began to migrate to the wilds of Kentucky in increasing numbers, igniting Indian wars that sometimes lasted for years. During that same time, the American War of Independence erupted, bringing nearly all of North America subject to engagement. At stake was a vast wilderness—with its fertile and untouched land—lying in North America on the frontiers of Kentucky and what was called the Ohio Country, including much of the Ohio River watershed, today occupied by several American states.

We'll now briefly review some of the geography that was around during one of the bloodiest and most agonizing periods of unrest in American history. It is also the geography that drew

Daniel Boone into a lifetime of adventure and difficulty.

Throughout the Revolutionary War, the lands comprising of what are now the states of Ohio, Illinois, Indiana, Michigan, Wisconsin, and part of Minnesota made up a giant wilderness area known as the Ohio Country. The Ohio Country boasted all the lands west of Pennsylvania and northwest of the Ohio River. At the start of the Revolutionary War, it was a part of the British Empire obtained from France in its treaty, ending the French and Indian War.

A British administrator out of Fort Detroit governed that large area of 260,000 square miles, and scattered forts—including Kaskaskia, Vincennes, and Cahokia, which were only lightly garrisoned—protected it. Those former forts are now thriving American cities that figured prominently in one of America's most daring and strategic victories. Even more impressive, perhaps, is the fact that the victory was planned, financed, and faultlessly executed by a young man named George Rogers Clark, an intrepid 25 year old, without firing a single shot.

The northwest wilderness had been in the making for nearly 20,000 years —ever since a giant ice sheet from the waning ice age decided to retreat to its home in the north, leaving behind a landscape of desolation for the forces of nature to reclaim. Before the war, Kentucky was unclaimed by whites, except for a few wanderers who fled

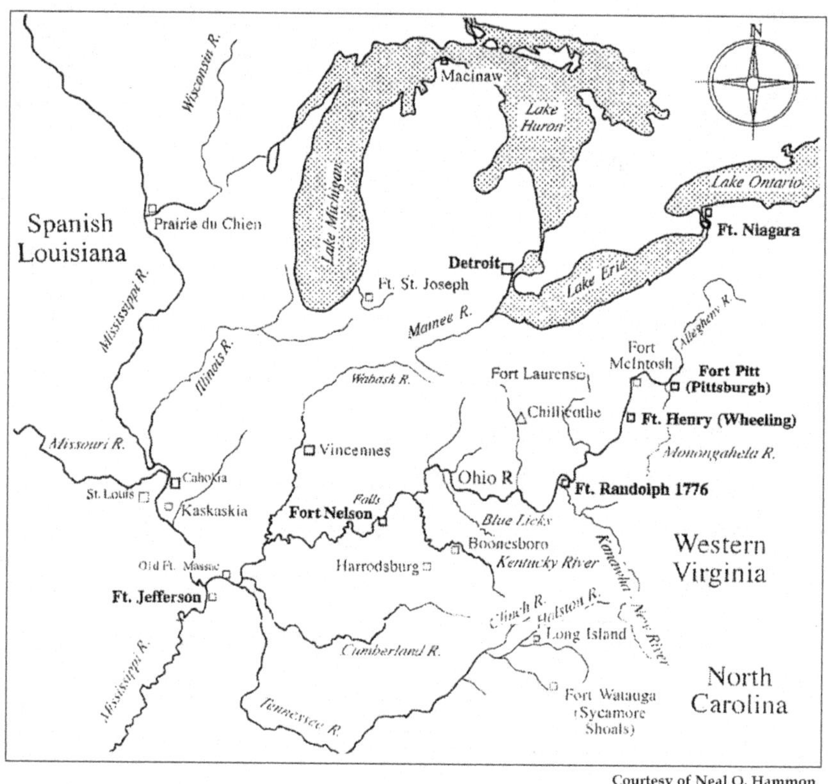

Courtesy of Neal O. Hammon

civilization in search of the riches rumored to be there; they also found a wild, ungoverned wilderness frequented by Indian warriors who coveted white scalps — and who were determined to have them.

Back then, the Ohio Country was home to approximately 45,000 Indians, scattered remnants of a once proud aboriginal culture that, for centuries, occupied most of North America before the coming of the white man, who brought with him the devastating pandemics of smallpox, tuberculosis, and venereal diseases that wiped out whole villages and decimated entire tribes.

Across the Ohio River to the south of the Ohio Country, only a few settlers occupied Kentucky. However, they soon fell victim to the tomahawks and scalping knives of the Indians who were also there. The Indians were fearful of the loss of their hunting grounds.

The Kentucky landscape that Daniel Boone first saw is still there for the most part. The geography and geology of Kentucky has undergone little change, and the stately mountains, broad flowing rivers, and the flora and fauna still thrive. A hiker can walk some of the same paths and climb the same mountains, float the same rivers and enjoy many of the same scenes that Daniel Boone and his companions saw over 250 years ago.

Kentucky was much like the Ohio Country. It was a vast wilderness with abundant game, ample forage, and hundreds of miles of rivers that coursed throughout the state, watering huge areas of meadows and canebrakes. It had forests with majestic trees that stood tall in black spongy soil—a huge compost deposit fed by leaves, limbs, and fallen tree trunks. Furthermore, it had herds of bison, grazing on bluegrass, which had only re-

Courtesy of Neal O. Hammon

cently found a proper place to set down its roots after migrating from some distant place. Kentucky was ready to share its bounty with anyone willing to brave its fierce challenges and the dangers it presented.

Kentucky was a hunting ground for the Indian tribes. They hunted buffalo, bear, and deer in abundance for food and furs. Over time, however, almost all of the Indian tribes left Kentucky and resettled in the lands to the north of the Ohio River. The Indians had no firm understanding of their ownership of that land. They considered Kentucky a hunting ground that was reserved exclusively for them, and they were resentful toward any trespassers upon those lands. It didn't matter if the newcomers were other hunters, settlers, explorers, or speculators.

A few hardy Europeans braved the wilderness and created small settlements, which led to the invitation of Indian attacks on the occupants of those homesteads. The marauding Indians often killed anyone they found in the course of those raids on the settlers, taking their scalps as trophies.

The few settlers who had succeeded in locating Kentucky found what they probably already knew — that Kentucky had no army or reliable militia able to protect them from Indian barbarities. If they decided to stay in Kentucky, they would be living in a state of virtual anarchy. Nevertheless, the few white men who saw Kentucky's landscape were drawn to it with dreams of riches, despite the fact that the land was inhospitable and unforgiving.

In the course of the Revolutionary War, Great Britain recruited Indians to make assaults upon settlements along the frontier, hoping to divert military assets of the colonies from the eastern battlefronts to the western settlements. Those raids were planned largely by the British and were carried out with the assistance of officers of the British military or paid mercenaries. The originator of the cruel strategy was Lieutenant Governor Henry Hamilton, the infamous so-called "Hair Buyer," who was stationed at Fort Detroit and commandant of the Ohio Country. One day, though, he would be called to give account for his callous use of the warring Indians.

The Indians who participated in those raids were often rewarded by payment of bounties on the scalps of innocent men, women, and children they found huddled in their crude shelters. Those raids were almost always launched from the British forts at Detroit, Kaskaskia, Cahokia, and Vincennes, or from one of the many neighboring Indian villages. Innocent victims of those incursions found the borders to be without any efficient defense, except for a voluntary militia, until a plan devised by the young George Rogers Clark was presented to and approved by a committee of the

Virginia Assembly to invade British forts of the Ohio Country. That plan was brilliantly and successfully carried out by recruitment of only 175 volunteers, most of whom were from the Kentucky settlements.

If the money and other assets used by the British over the course of the war could be calculated, there is little doubt that more assets were diverted from the British cause over the five years of the Indian operation than were diverted from the cause of the colonies.

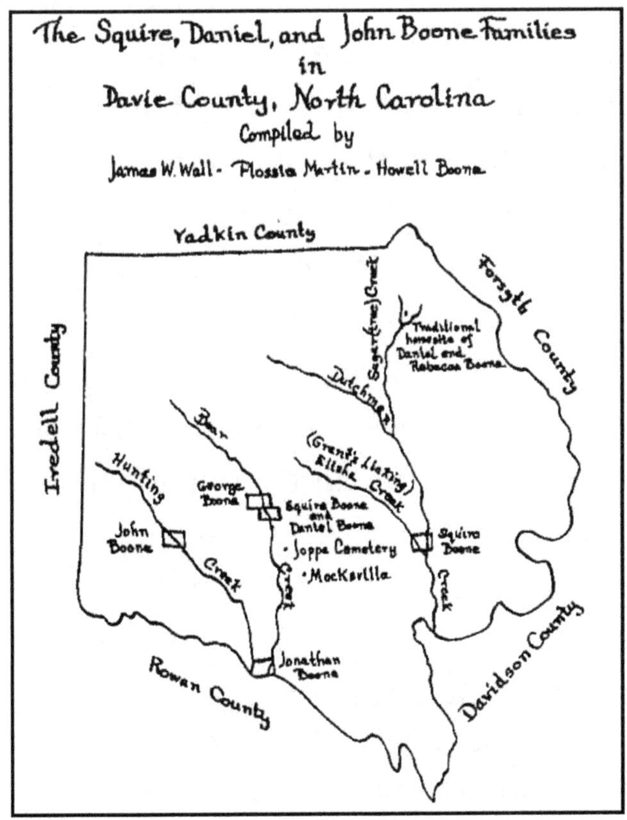

1
Move 'Em Out

"All the religion I have is to love and fear God, do all the good to my neighbors and myself that I can, do as little harm as I can help, and trust on God's mercy for the rest." —Colonel Daniel Boone

In 1748, Squire Boone, Sr., Daniel's father, was excommunicated and stripped of membership of the Pennsylvania Quaker church he and his family attended by the Exeter Society of Friends. Before being expelled from fellowship, Squire and his wife, Sarah, had been faithful members of that church; in fact, Squire had even held several offices and trusts. The Boones were shocked when, in two separate church proceedings, two of their children were noticed by the church for separate infractions against the Exeter Society of Friends, calling for repentance and apologies. The Boones thought that the proceedings were an outrage.

In the first proceeding, their oldest child, Sarah, had married John Willcoxon outside of the

Quaker faith. The proceeding later revealed that she was pregnant at the time they married. Squire and his wife made the necessary confessions and apologies, and were excused from discipline and expulsion. However, the daughter was required to read a public confession and then was expelled. The church's actions caused the Boone family considerable grief and embarrassment. But the matter was eventually settled, and the family grudgingly accepted the results.

Another conflict arose later, which had a far greater impact on the Boone family and their relationship with the Quakers. The second oldest child, Israel, married a "worldling" in a ceremony that wasn't consistent with the Quaker tradition. Squire and his wife were again called to answer the second complaint. This time, however, Squire was not so contrite. He stood his ground on behalf of Israel on a charge that he considered inconsequential.

He refused to acknowledge that the union of his son with a woman outside of the Quaker faith justified expulsion, and he refused to make the required apology, contending that the young people involved should have the right and privilege to marry whomever they wanted. His remonstrations in an angry letter to the Exeter Society of Friends were deemed so vitriolic that the clerk refused to enter them into the church records. That seemed to have concluded the matter. After that incident, though, Squire was expelled. He spent the rest of his life away from the Quaker fellowship, and his feelings of resentment never faded. Regardless of what his children ever did, he would always be ready to come to their defense if they needed him.

Squire was a slight but steady man with red hair, gray eyes, and fair skin. A farmer, weaver, and blacksmith, he married Sarah Morgan in a ceremony on September 23, 1720. His new wife was somewhat larger than most women of the time, and she had dark eyes and black hair. The Boones' thirty-year marriage produced eleven children, almost one every two years.

Like some of his neighbors, Squire was concerned that the soil in the Oley, Pennsylvania, area had become so depleted from years of farming that they were no longer fertile enough to produce crops and grasslands as they had when he bought them. He knew that if he wanted to continue farming, he would have to move his family to a place where soil was richer and more productive. Dozens of northeastern farmers apparently had the same concern, and they began moving their families toward the rich and fertile lands of Virginia,

North Carolina, and locales further south. They'd sometimes stop along the way to tell others about the opportunities thought to be available in those places.

There is no way to know for sure, but the resourceful Squire had probably heard of the Yadkin Valley in North Carolina, which made up a good part of that colony. His bother-in-law, Joseph Stover, who had moved to a new home near the Shenandoah River in Linville, Virginia, had given him glowing accounts of the countryside and related to him that there was land in both Virginia and North Carolina that could be bought by any man who had a horse, a rifle, and a good woman. He may have even have mentioned the fertile Yadkin Valley as one place to consider in any move the Boone family might make.

In 1750, Squire was still smarting from the unfair action taken against him, his wife, and his two children two years earlier. It had left him embarrassed and without a church to attend. But Squire was in his fifties, and that was no age to pick up and move an entire family. He and Sarah spent many hours going over what it would mean to sell their land, their gristmill, their cattle, and even dispose of their weaving business. In the end, the arguments for leaving were compelling. It seemed like a good time to investigate the virgin lands that were opening up in several areas to the south.

Finally, a decision to move was made, and a May 1, 1750, departure date was officially set. This would be a decision that would affect the whole Boone family for years to come, particularly young Daniel. Squire and Sarah sold their Oley homestead for a little more than 300 pounds to a cousin, which they thought was enough money to set themselves up in a new area, according to other travelers. They were not sure where they would settle, but they knew it would be somewhere on the western frontier where fertile land was plentiful and could be bought at a reasonable price.

Plans for the big move were in the making for several weeks. Sarah spent numerous hours in the kitchen, making beef jerky, drying vegetables, and putting together other things the family would need for the journey down the Old Wagon Road. She and Squire had told Daniel, only sixteen years old, that he would travel in the forefront of the entourage. From that position, he would be responsible for killing any animals that might stray across their path as they made their way toward their destination; they could use the animals for food later.

Daniel already owned some of the equipment

used by hunters in their hunts. He had also already adopted for life the single braid worn by the Indians around Oley, whose hunting skills he had come to admire. They had often taken him on hunts of their own. Daniel wasn't the only Boone child with a task while the family took their journey. All of the older children were probably given chores to do in preparation for the expedition—gathering firewood, carrying water, and feeding the animals—as well as during it.

Squire made sure that everything the family might need was packed away in the large wagons, including food, pry bars, gunsmith tools, shovels, and scores of other implements that would be needed to ready the new land for crops. Squire, who was also a gunsmith, had provided rifles that would be used to fend off any attacks from the growing number of robbers that they heard were regularly harassing travelers along the Old Wagon Road.

Arising early on May 1, Squire felt the warm May sun and looked across at the meadows. They were beginning to take on the yellows and greens of a new spring season. It was the time when he usually plowed and cultivated his fields for the new crop. It definitely was not the time for a fifty-year-old man with all those children to pull up roots and move his family to a place they had never seen—but that's exactly what he was about to do.

He remembered how his land had looked when he and Sarah first bought it. Most of it was covered with trees and underbrush that the previous owner had left for someone else to clear. With the help of his growing family and neighbors, he had cleared the fertile land, dug stumps, chopped away underbrush, and moved hundreds of stones that had dotted the fields. It was backbreaking work, but it had to be done. The new ground could be cultivated and put into crop only after it had been properly cleared, and tangled tree roots and brush had been removed or rotted away.

The entourage included large wagons, each with a team of draft horses to pull them up and down the sometimes steep and muddy roads. Squire loaded up the draft horses with furniture and baskets that he carefully strapped to their backs. Then he packed the last of the family's plunder onto the largest wagon. Once he could no longer add anything else to the wagons, he took the leftover items and put them into a pile. He then set the pile on fire and watched as the flames ate away the last of the family's time in the Oley community.

He checked the harnesses of the horses on

each wagon to be sure that they were properly buckled and made ready for the trip south. After the travelers had taken their places, he probably strolled to the front of the lead wagon and began stroking the horses and pulling their manes, exhorting them to begin moving forward. The wagon made a painful sigh, moving reluctantly toward a place the excited family had never seen.

Daniel, traveling at the front of the caravan, was followed by Squire, Sarah, and their eight unmarried children, including Squire, Jr. The children's ages ranged from three to nineteen years old. The full group included a granddaughter, the married daughter, Sarah, her husband, and their baby, as well as two sons and their wives. A grown nephew, Henry Miller, Daniel's best friend, and some members of Squire's extended family also joined the group. Altogether, twenty-one people made the journey southward. The move probably followed the Old Wagon Road, which, for centuries, was the preferred route for the Scotch, Irish, and German immigrants who traveled from Pennsylvania to the rich lands of Virginia, North Carolina, and South Carolina.

The first stage of the journey took the party due west. The remaining trip required them to cross various rivers, streams, fords, and other obstacles; however, that was the principal migration route for travelers going to the southern back-countries. The road leading to where Joseph Stover lived, while remote and treacherous in some sections, was not as difficult as they thought it might be.

When the caravan stopped for the evenings, a fire was quickly built, and roasted slabs of venison or wild turkey that young Daniel had skillfully taken from his forward position would be cooked. During the day, the group chewed on beef jerky or smoked venison from the night before. They always tried to camp somewhere where Sarah could easily wash, rinse, and dry clothing for the travelers.

But the traveling life was not always pleasurable. The group probably encountered mud that caused the wagons to sink all the way down to the hub, sometimes requiring hours to extricate them after first unloading the entire cargo. At other times, they endured discomforts, including swarms of stinging insects that would make the younger children cry. If rivers could not be forded, they had to wait for ferries to take them across. Furthermore, Sarah was concerned for their safety from robbers. For this reason, the men were always prepared with Pennsylvania long rifles to defend themselves against anyone wishing to test them.

If the Boones spent two years in Linville on the Shenandoah River, they probably didn't spend much of that time watching the corn grow. Squire had achieved a measure of prosperity from his successes as a businessman. He was looking for a place with fertile soil, ample water, and other things a good farmer would look for to pass on to his children. He knew that he could not find that in a bean patch. He was ready to spend considerable money that had been slowly accumulated during the thirty years of his marriage to Sarah. But he was not about to spend it without knowing what he was getting for the price.

It must have been common knowledge that Earl Granville had a huge tract of virgin land in North Carolina, which was called the Yadkin Valley. The Crown had granted him the land. He had sold portions of that property to enterprising buyers at reasonable prices—the first purchase being eight years earlier in 1742. Later in 1748, an Irish settlement, populated by Scotish-Irish migrants, bought property in Rowan County. During only 21 years between 1749 and 1770, the Yadkin Valley would grow from an uninhabited wilderness area to a well-settled district, with towns in

Salem and Salisbury. If Squire decided to buy property in the Yadkin Valley, he would be among its first settlers. He had enough money from the sale of their Pennsylvania property to resettle, whether in North Carolina or anywhere else he might find.

With only part of the money from the sale of the Pennsylvania homestead, Squire decided to buy a square mile of land on Dutchman's Creek, which flows into the Yadkin River at Buffalo Lick. He was delighted by his purchase. With that, he continued to buy property from Earl Granville until he owned approximately three square miles of choice wilderness, quickly becoming one of the largest landowners in the Yadkin Valley.

2
Daniel on the Yadkin

"The settling of this region well deserves a place in history. Most of the memorable events I have myself been exercised in; and, for the satisfaction of the public, will briefly relate the circumstances of my adventures, and scenes of life, from my first movement to this country until this day."—Colonel Daniel Boone

By 1750, things were already happening in the Yadkin Valley. People throughout the American colonies were on the move, looking for ways to better themselves. They wanted a share of the new lands that were opening up.

Governor Johnson recognized the potential for growth and development in the Yadkin Valley in a statement he made to the Board of Trade on February 15, 1750:

"... Inhabitants flock in here daily, most from Pennsylvania and other parts of America, who are overstocked with people and some directly from Europe. They commonly seat themselves toward the west and have got near the mountains."

In another statement to the Board of Trade on June 28, 1753, Governor Pro-Tem Matthew Riley wrote:

> "In the year 1746, I was in the Country that is now Anson, Orange, and Rowan Countys. There was not then above 100 fighting men: there is now at least three thousand for the most part Irish Protestants and Germans, and daily increasing."

In April 1753, the Colonial Assembly selected a small town called Salisbury to serve as the county seat of Rowan by the Colonial Assembly. It would soon provide citizens of the Yadkin Valley with a new courthouse and jail. The construction of a courthouse signaled an expansion, and Squire must have been impressed with the building of a center for government in the middle of what was essentially vast wilderness.

Most of the first settlers were from the colonies. Many of them had been forced to move because of the high cost and scarcity of land, which made it difficult to buy their own. They were hardworking people on the lookout for ways to better themselves and their families. Those from foreign countries were ethnically diverse, mostly Scotch-Irish and German.

Prior to the Revolution, all areas of North Carolina were subject to laws and processes imposed by the Crown through His Majesty's colonial government. The colonies enjoyed the military protection of English regulars and militia. There were scattered towns where the hearty settlers could take their furs, farm produce, and other properties to sell and return with the necessities that they had to have in order to survive on the rugged new land.

Salisbury was the nearest town to where Squire and his family had purchased land. Its settlers could gather around for conversation, competitions with firearms, and other such activities. Even on the remote Yadkin River, there were fragments of civilization, destined to expand with the arrival of the many migrants who had decided to test the pristine wilderness. Salisbury was not much different from any other frontier town that was isolated from civilization. It had been described by settlers as unruly and sometimes wild.

When Daniel first saw the Yadkin Valley, he must have felt at home with his destiny. A short walk would take him from the family cabin into the wilderness. He could learn the habits of nature and her children; the wilderness was a venue that would ultimately become Daniel's classroom. It was where he would spend so much of his life.

Any story of Daniel's life must include the Yadkin and the things that he found there, as well as the people he met and all the things he experienced that made him who he was. Many of his companions on his long hunts were friends and neighbors whom he had met on the Yadkin—people like Benjamin Cutbirth, husband of a niece; Michael Stoner, who became a lifelong friend, and various long hunters and Indian fighters. All of these folks were friends and neighbors whom he would build his life around, and whose names would be associated with him in the telling of his story. Everywhere life sent Daniel, whether through the Cumberland Gap, down the Ohio River, or on the Warrior's Path, he took pieces of the Yadkin Valley with him. Ultimately, it was a part of who he would become.

When Squire bought into the Yadkin Valley, there was still plenty of land and habitat to support wildlife. The valley had several varieties of first-growth timber, mostly along the river bottom, and other vegetation. One observer, who passed through the Yadkin Valley countryside while it was still relatively unsettled, wrote:

"The soil was exceedingly rich on both

sides, abounding in rank grass and pro-digiously large trees, and for plenty of fish, fowl, and venison is inferior to no part of the northern continent. There the traders commonly lie still for some days, to recruit their horses' flesh, as well as to recover their own spirits."

Daniel's hunting academy was not yet ready to shut down, and most of the hunting he did during the next four years was for pleasure. He would often take the short musket that Squire had given him when he was 13 years old into places where game was plentiful. Then he would proudly harvest skins and furs and sell them in Salisbury.

However, deer, bear, and other game were on most settlers' menus, and the valley became so intensely hunted that Daniel soon had to venture out farther and farther to find any. That meant returning with heavier and more bulky bundles of skins and furs. Longer hunts required more provisions, and the list of supplies grew longer while the cost became more expensive. Daniel was on his way to becoming a long hunter, not so much by choice as by necessity.

By the time he was twenty, Daniel had become a professional hunter. His marksmanship was excellent, and he traveled hours through the woods, across rocks, mud, rivers, briars, and brush without any difficulty. He had come to enjoy the solitude that is the life of a hunter. He had learned the habits of his prey. Unlike many other hunters on the prairie, Daniel had also come to respect the Indian culture; he worked hard to build on that relationship. He had adopted the Indians' manner of dress, and he even wore his long hair in an Indian-style single braid.

Daniel had grown into a strong young man, weighing approximately 175 pounds and built like a horse. He was said to have had pronounced facial features with a high forehead, heavy brow, prominent cheekbones, and long, slender limbs. He had inherited his father's blue eyes and ruddy complexion and his mother's dark hair.

In Salisbury, Daniel often engaged in shooting matches that offered rifles, turkeys, and other prizes, and sometimes the right to collect lead around the target area. He was always ready to compete and nearly always won the prize. He even began performing trick shots. The locals in and around the courthouse were delighted with Daniel's ability to point his rifle at the target with one hand and actually hit the target, too.

Yadkin Valley settlers had been spared the Indian warfare that had been endured by other settlers in other parts of the new world. The Catawbas were domiciled about sixty miles from

Salisbury, and the Cherokees were even farther away. The Indians often visited the new settlement, curious of the new arrivals and their ways. They came to barter and trade with their white neighbors. On one occasion, when a party of northern Indians showed up in Rowan County and committed acts of scattered violence, a band of friendly Catawbas suddenly appeared, killing several of the intruders and chasing the others away. However, they first took valuables from the surprised Indians, relieving them of their scalps and other treasures, and bearing signs that they had been manufactured in France.

Daniel may never have seen a hostile Indian before moving to the Yadkin Valley. In Exeter, the Indians had traveled a long way toward pacification and had adopted many aspects of the white man's culture, making it easier to live among them in peace. In Salisbury, where he sometimes went on legal business, Daniel met many men of influence.

Judge Richard Henderson, a lawyer of the local bar, and a judge of the Colonial Courts who had authored the Transylvania purchase of Kentucky, had profoundly influenced Daniel's life. Daniel's father was eventually appointed one of the judges of the County Court of Pleas and Quarter Sessions where Judge Henderson sat. Then there were John Williams, a lawyer and business associate of Judge Henderson, and Thomas Harp, the sheriff of Orange County. These were men with power who listened carefully to Daniel's descriptions of the landscape to the west that he had seen while hunting in the wilderness. Daniel respected them all.

After the Boones settled on their land and started tending it, they became acquainted with a family of Bryans, whose clan had taken up residence ten miles to the north of the forest. The mother, Martha, died at the age of sixty. Two years later, the father brought his sons and daughters into the Yadkin Valley where he bought large tracts of property. He planned to eventually divide the land between his descendents. That property became known as the Bryan Settlement.

The Bryan father became the owner of thousands of acres of property, which was more than anyone else owned in the whole back country. Three years after the Boone family arrived in Yadkin Valley, Squire's 16 year old daughter married a Bryan son. Squire's nephew, John, married a Bryan daughter, Rebecca. Thus began a family line that would continue for several generations.

For several years before the Boones settled in the Yadkin Valley, trouble developed between the

English, the French, and their sometimes-Indian allies over competing claims to parts of the Ohio Valley. The claims were asserted at various times by battles and skirmishes that eventually escalated into open warfare. In the course of long hostilities, neither side was able to inflict decisive losses upon the other, and so the war dragged on. When London received shocking news of the loss of two important battles, the British government, after several months of argument and negotiations within, decided to send in an army to North America to finally and decisively defeat the French.

Major General Edward Braddock was chosen to lead the expedition; however, even before he left for North America, the British plans were leaked to France, causing the country to dispatch six regiments to the colonies. A planned blockade of the French fleet and capture by the British of two French ships led to a formal declaration of war between the French and English in the spring of 1756. Major General Braddock decided to then lead a mission to Fort Duquesne and consider other operations against other installations. He began his campaign to take Fort Duquesne in June 1755.

Around the same time, Daniel decided to enlist as a wagoneer, and he soon met some impress-ive men. The person in charge of the commissary was Dr. Thomas Walker, one of the early explorers who probably knew more about the mysterious Kentucky wilderness than any other man. A lead-ing scout was Christopher Gist, a veteran woods-man, who had also been George Washington's guide and a neighbor of the Boones in the Yadkin Valley. John Finley, who had recently returned from a trading trip to Kentucky, was another wa-goneer with the expedition.

It was providential that these four men should find themselves at the same place at the same time. Dr. Walker had been the first settler to discover the Cumberland Gap, the Narrows, and the Cumber-land Crossing in 1750. Additionally, he had led a group of explorers into Kentucky. John had recent-ly returned from trading with the Indians and had caught a glimpse of the Kentucky landscape from an Indian trading village near the Kentucky River. He was particularly interested in a path the Indi-ans used to gain access to Kentucky from the North; he wondered if that pathway did not con-tinue through Kentucky to a gap or a breach in the towering mountains.

Whatever happened around those campfires, both Daniel and John went away with visions of a

Kentucky that was rich beyond anything they had ever seen. John most likely described what he had seen of Kentucky during his short sojourn there and later referred to it as a "good speck." These conversations would come to have a profound impact on Daniel's life.

Major General Braddock's expedition was in jeopardy from the start, and it would go down in history as one of Britain's greatest military disasters. Although the British had a far superior military force, their regulars were unaccustomed to Indian warfare. The British were unable to overcome the French and Indian defenders and were thrown into disarray.

Meanwhile, Daniel, in control of his supply wagon, saw the flight of the British force and its inevitable defeat. Unable to extricate his wagon from the turmoil of flight, he and his fellow wagoneers—being in the rear of the action and unable to flee—cut their traces and rode for their lives. Some wagoneers were killed, but Daniel and John escaped. There was nothing for Daniel to do but ride his horse to safety and limp homeward as a different man.

During the war, the Yadkin Valley was attacked in a number of Indian raids at the urging of the French. The attacks came from tribes north of the Ohio River, as well as tribes to the south of Yadkin

Valley—notably the unpredictable Cherokees. Because of the anxiety caused by the war and the threat of Indian attacks, people living in the Yadkin Valley were encouraged to build protective forts or stations. Other tribes drawn from north of the Ohio River killed several settlers along the border between North Carolina and Virginia. Cherokee Indians, with grievances of their own, raided farms, destroyed crops, and killed and injured residents. Stories of the attacks provoked even more fear, and many people of the Bryan Settlement fled to the protective forts and other places where Indian attacks could be repelled.

After Major General Braddock's defeat—and because of Indian uprisings in the Yadkin Valley—there soon began a troubling migration of frightened people who were all trying to escape raids against settlements in the Yadkin Valley. People, including George Washington, expressed their fear that whole counties would be emptied because the back settlements were fleeing to the southern colonies. Armed patrols were dispatched to protect the settlements in Rowan County. However, the Indians committed many deprecations upon the settlements. Any that didn't have forts to protect them would ultimately be destroyed.

During that tumultuous period, the Boone

family temporarily moved to Virginia and other safer locations, reducing their exposure to the violence being committed upon the Yadkin Valley. That's when Daniel began working as a teamster in Virginia, hauling tobacco to market and bringing supplies back to the colony. He also performed military services at various times before a treaty with the Indians effectively ended combat, and the Yadkin Valley lapsed into a welcomed peace.

In the summer of 1755, Daniel began to notice Rebecca Bryan, daughter of the Boone family's neighbor, Morgan Bryan. By that time, the Boone family had moved close to the Bryans, both families living in the Yadkin Valley again. Squire and Morgan had both been appointed as justices of the peace for the County Court, and they had come to enjoy a close relationship that would last for generations. It was no wonder that the young Daniel was attracted to Rebecca. She was once described as an extremely pretty woman who was apparently oversized and well-endowed. She was said to be well-behaved, mild of temper, and pleasant of speech. Furthermore, a Quaker by habit, she was careful to always keep a tidy house.

In Squire's position as a justice of the peace, he performed the marriage ceremony between Daniel and Rebecca on August 14, 1756. Daniel was 21;

Rebecca was 17. After the wedding ceremony, the bride and groom were subjected to the usual mock post-wedding serenade, including jokes, being escorted to the loft, and then being thrown into their bed to consummate their marriage once everyone left. Before all of that, the bride's sisters had prepared a feast with plenty to eat and jugs of strong whiskey.

For the new Rebecca Bryan Boone, there was no cruise to Barbados for a honeymoon. Instead, she immediately took over the responsibility of raising the children of Daniel's brother, Israel, who had died two months earlier. The boys, Jessie and Jonathan, continued to live with Rebecca and the family in North Carolina until 1773, when the family left for Kentucky. In May 1757, Rebecca had her first child, born nine months after the wedding. A second son, Israel, was born twenty months later. Not yet twenty years old, Rebecca was nurturing four children and, over the course of her marriage to Daniel, would deliver a total of ten children, separated by only an average of two-and-a-half years.

For a wife and mother like Rebecca, her work schedule was not measured by minutes and hours. Her responsibilities were myriad and included cooking, washing, sewing, cleaning, weaving, carrying water, chopping wood, hoeing gardens, milking cows, keeping gardens, harvesting, mothering the children, and doing other things that a modern-day wife would not think of undertaking. Rebecca had all of that responsibility at a time when she was pregnant and having to tend to chores at the same time.

What is impressive is not only the scope of the work that she was required to do, but also that she did it throughout her entire life. She is not reported as ever having complained about Daniel's absence, the debts that would plague him throughout their marriage, or any of the responsibilities marriage had imposed upon her. The most amazing thing of all is that Rebecca remained at home alone while this man of the wilderness remained gone for years at a time, not knowing whether he was dead or alive, or if she would ever see him again.

3
Call of the Wild

"It was on the first of May, in the year 1769, that I resigned my domestic happiness for a time, and left my family and peaceable habitation on the Yadkin River, in North-Carolina, to wander through the wilderness of America, in quest of the country of Kentucke ..."—Colonel Daniel Boone

Before the birth of their first child, Daniel and Rebecca moved from their first home—a cabin on Squire's land—to a small farm in the Bryan Settlement where they lived for almost ten years. During that decade, Daniel earned money for his family through various jobs, including farming, working as a blacksmith, and hauling supplies back and forth to the county seat. However, he mostly earned a living by hunting and trapping. After the harvest was in, he fell to hunting the broad expanse of wilderness, streams, and cane-brakes. Short hunts lasted a few hours, requiring him to sit in deer stands. Long hunts took him away from home for weeks or months at a time. The more settled the Yadkin Valley became, the further west into the Appalachian wilderness Daniel had to go to find anything, keeping him away from Rebecca for longer periods of time.

On one occasion in 1760, when Daniel was on a long hunt, he and another companion met an African-American who told them about hunting expeditions in the Blue Ridge, an area easily accessible through a road laid down by the hooves of buffalo herds. The old hunter then led Daniel and his companion to a cabin located high in the meadow. Following the Indians' path, they encountered a commanding view of the Appalachian Mountains.

The hunters spent the winter trapping and hunting in North Carolina, the eastern part of Tennessee, and the southwestern part of Virginia. The cabin they used was used several times by Daniel in subsequent hunts in that area. During that period, he and other hunters from the Yadkin Valley explored the wilderness and set up hunts in other areas that were accessible to the Yadkin River. Daniel would sometimes spend months with no hunting companion other than a horse or a dog. He had a decided preference for hunting and tracking alone. He preferred solitude to the companionship of others, and sometimes had books to read, including his favorite novel by Jonathan Swift, Gulliver's Travels. Indians were often near, though, and sometimes caused Daniel to seek refuge in cane patches, caves, and other hiding places.

There were times, however, when Daniel wished he had brought a companion along. One time when he was by himself, hunting near the present Jonesborough, Tennessee, on a winter night, Cherokee hunters encircled his camp. When he awoke, he relied on his knowledge of the woods and his familiarity with Indian customs and practices to escape a fearsome situation. He looked straight at the Indians and addressed them in a friendly way while smiling, showing no fear. Since he was hunting in Cherokee territory, the threat of harm was substantial. He was not outwardly intimidated but welcomed the Indians as guests. It is likely that he offered the Indians a drink from his flask. The whole ordeal ended with Daniel being released unharmed but relieved of the considerable cache of furs and skins that he had taken from the Indians' preferred hunting territory.

The Cherokee War was responsible for separating Daniel from his family for almost two years. Imagine his astonishment when he finally returned home to find that his family had grown by one more child, Jemima. Records indicate that Jemima was born on October 4, 1762—more than nine months since Daniel had been away.

Naturally, Daniel assumed that she had been conceived during his absence. When he confronted Rebecca about the dilemma, she replied, "You should have been here, Boone!" Upon finding out that he had been betrayed by his brother, he shrugged his shoulders and reportedly said, "Oh, well. It's in the family." That is only one of the several versions of that conversation. [Is it fair to ask whether there was any apology from the brother who betrayed Daniel?]

Daniel faced a recurring problem as he entered his thirties. The population of the Yadkin Valley continued to grow. The increased settlement resulted in a reduction in game, making commercial hunting all the more difficult so that Daniel regularly found himself unable to meet his obligations. His creditors often took him to court for his debts. During his epic trip to Kentucky, Daniel's financial troubles had grown so big that when the County Court of Rowan County entered judgment against him for the large sum of fifty pounds, he may have paid through the sale of property given to him by his father. The sale of that patrimony left Daniel without other land in the forks. Adding to his financial problems was Daniel's grief over Squire's death on August 22, 1765. That was a time of great disappointment and discontent in Daniel's life.

We do not know what the relationship between Squire and Daniel was like during Squire's latter years, and the question arises whether Daniel and his father got along. Squire was a hard-working, frugal man. He was also a devoted father. He was a good citizen and a justice in the court of law, and he seemed to always have his children in mind. The same cannot be said for Daniel. His neighbors criticized him for his long absences from home, leaving his family alone. It could be inferred that his father was equally critical of his son's truancy from his domestic responsibilities.

Biographers have said much about Daniel's repetitive dreams after the death of his father in which he saw Squire sometimes appearing pleasant but often angry. Those dreams were sometimes attended by nightmares. It could be suggested that they were expressions of inner remorse over his repeated absences from his family, his ever present debt obligations, and his loss of patrimony. Squire is known for his devotion to his family, hard work, and responsibility. He might have expected the same from his son and the father of his grandchildren.

What we do know about Daniel is that from the time he married Rebecca, he was almost always in debt and the defendant in many actions in the Rowan County Court. He disliked common labor like gardening, taking care of the cattle, and other chores relating to farming. Instead, he would go off and spend as much as two years on hunting trips, leaving his wife and children to fend for themselves. He was constantly on the move from a poorly located cabin to an even worse cabin on rocky soil, which made Rebecca's work more difficult. Daniel had proposed to Rebecca that they move into the Blue Ridge Mountains at a place near the Proclamation Line of 1763, which restricted migrants from settling beyond that point. That location was so remote and so isolated that Rebecca refused to make the move.

With the suspension of the Indian conflicts, the Yadkin Valley continued to grow, bringing with it increased settlement accompanied by an even greater increase in Daniel's debts. One lawyer observed that Daniel had more lawsuits against him than any other person in the Yadkin Valley. During that time, Daniel was living with Rebecca and his children in a cabin removed from the Bryan and Boone settlements.

The remote Blue Ridge Mountains offered good hunting, but Daniel heard increasing talk about the land to the west, which came to be known as Kentucky. He remembered he had heard from a fellow wagoneer—the Irishman, John Finley—glowing stories of the splendor of Kentucky as they sat by their campfires, waiting to engage the French and Indian enemies fourteen years earlier. John related how, as a trader, he had recently visited the Blue Lick Town where he traded furs and skins of excellent quality. He told Daniel that Kentucky was a land of cane and clover with fertile lands, profuse game, and trade opportunities—altogether a "good speck." Daniel had been so charmed by the description that he decided he would someday go to Kentucky.

He became increasingly impatient with colonial restraints against settlement into the western grounds of Kentucky, which deprived him of the game that he desperately needed to find to carry on his hunting. The mountains of Kentucky and western North Carolina were physical impediments to further exploration; however, they seemed only to challenge his sense of adventure and curiosity. Daniel knew that the country beyond those mountains would conceal Indians whose love of war would fuel their anger at any encroachment on their hunting grounds. In spite of all of the obstacles before him, he was determined to someday answer the call of the mysterious Kentucky.

But it was not until twelve years later, during the winter of 1767 and 1768, that Daniel finally decided to explore Kentucky. William Hill, a friend and splendid backwoodsman, his brother, Squire, Jr., and three other unnamed adventurers joined Daniel in the long hunt. They hunted around the Clinch River, crossed the Appalachian Ridge to the Big Sandy River, and followed various river courses to present day Prestonsburg, Kentucky. Once there, they encountered a heavy snowstorm and remained where they were for the entire winter. When weather permitted, Daniel and his companions returned to the upper Yadkin, having encountered game, including bison. On that particular hunt, Daniel was introduced to bison tongue, liver, and roast hump. The area Daniel and his companions covered by that hunt—being mountainous and extremely inaccessible—did not justify the glowing reports of the Kentucky that John had described to the wagoneers, and Daniel had no interest in pursuing it further.

Later in 1768, Benjamin Cutbirth, a twenty-eight-year-old hunter and friend of Daniel's with whom he had often hunted and who was the husband of his niece, set out from the Yadkin Valley on an extended adventure. He was in search of more bountiful game. Benjamin was a very quiet man, well-suited for the long hunting trips that Daniel and the other hunters in the Yadkin Valley were accustomed to making. He was a man of strong mind and body, and not very communicative—all traits shared by Daniel.

Benjamin recruited three young men from the Yadkin Valley—John Stewart, John Baker, and John Ward—to accompany him on his trip, but he did not invite Daniel. The journey took the four men westward along a little known Indian Trail that crossed the Appalachian Mountains, and they hunted along what is now the Kentucky and Tennessee border. After a rather successful hunt, during which they gathered many furs and skins, the group reached the Mississippi River. They were the first white men to accomplish the feat while traveling over land. The group then made it to New Orleans where the men sold their furs, skins, and meat for good prices. On their return home, the group headed back home through what was then Indian territory and what are now the states of Alabama and Mississippi.

Their success, however, was short-lived. A group of Choctaws, or Creek Indians, approached them and robbed them of everything they had. When the hunters finally reached home, completely broke, they vowed that they would never repeat the journey. They must have described to Daniel what they had encountered, though, and told him of the plentiful game that they had taken. Daniel reproached himself for not joining in the expedition, but somehow convinced himself that he had not been asked to go because he was too old. Either way, Benjamin's Mississippi trip may have rekindled Daniel's interest in the journey to Kentucky, and he was determined to provision another long hunt, taking along John Stewart, one of his favorite hunting companions.

Fourteen years had passed since John Finley first told Daniel what he might find to the west and beyond the mountains. But one day, by design or happenstance, John stood in Daniel's modest cabin with Daniel, Squire, Jr., Rebecca, and all of the children probably gathered around the fireplace, gravely recalling in his Irish brogue the Major General Braddock defeat and how close they had come to becoming casualties that day. John also reminded Daniel of those nights around the campfires when they discussed the mysteries of Kentucky and the vast forests, canebrakes, and other landscapes to be found there.

John had visited Daniel and his family because he wanted to explore Kentucky and proposed to his longtime friend that they do it together. John kept referring to Kentucky or at least the parts that he saw as a "good speck." Maybe he saw Kentucky as a good place to develop a trade in furs and other Indian goods. Daniel must have told him about his effort to enter Kentucky through the mountains two years earlier, and about how he and his companions had encountered a severe snowstorm, which led to them staying there the entire winter. He told John that they saw plenty of game while they were on their hunt, but that the difficulties they had come across in the mountainous terrain kept the trip from being worthwhile.

Others had already tried to reach the interior of Kentucky from the south. The most notable person had been Dr. Thomas Walker, who had explored for the Loyal Company and discovered and named the Cumberland Gap in 1750. His expedition did not find an acceptable route to the interior because the mountain barriers on the route he took made it impracticable. But John claimed to have an idea. Nobody on record had entered Kentucky from the Cumberland Gap and followed the Warrior's Path to its terminus in the north. Why not put together an expedition and test his idea that such a route already existed? It would enable migrants to enter Kentucky from Virginia, North Carolina, and other areas south. It would also avoid the arduous trip by way of the Ohio River.

One can imagine this small group sitting by the fire in Daniel's cabin, perhaps sipping jars of homemade spirits to free their minds and lubricate their tongues, growing more and more excited and animated at the thought of being among the first to see it — to make history. John made it clear that he needed a guide and a woodsman who was experienced in wilderness life. He figured there would be no shortage of men wanting to join the hunt because hunters in the Yadkin Valley were having difficulty supporting themselves with the shortage of game in their usual hunting areas. It was probably agreed that they should not delay because the coming spring was a good time to mount the assault upon the uncharted wilderness. They would need to recruit early from among the other hunters in the Yadkin Valley before the best gamesmen committed to other hunts.

With a general plan in place, the men soon saddled their horses and made their way to the homes of other hunters whom they had agreed to take along. They would provision themselves with things they knew they would need. The journey would require as many as fifteen horses, saddles, halters, and other leather equipment. They would need bear bacon, beef jerky, and other items to supplement the food they would kill along the way. All in all, there was much work to be done before they could even consider leaving the Yadkin Valley for the great mysteries to be found beyond the Big Sandy.

On May 1, 1769, Daniel Boone, John Finley, John Stewart, Joseph Holden, James Monay, and William Cooley mounted their horses and left to "wander through the wilderness of America in quest of the center of Kentucky." It must have been exciting, not only for the hunters, but also for the families, neighbors, and friends from all over the Yadkin Valley.

The men had with them the supplies needed by hunters of that day, developed through years of living in the wilderness. They preferred wide brimmed felt hats, long homespun shirts, buckskin leggings over linen breeches, and moccasins. They each had a Pennsylvania long rifle, a powder horn, and a bullet pouch. Daniel, of course, carried a sheathed hunting knife and a tomahawk carefully tucked in his belt. On their packhorses, they carried traps, kettles, smithing tools, and extra rifles, powder, shot, and flints.

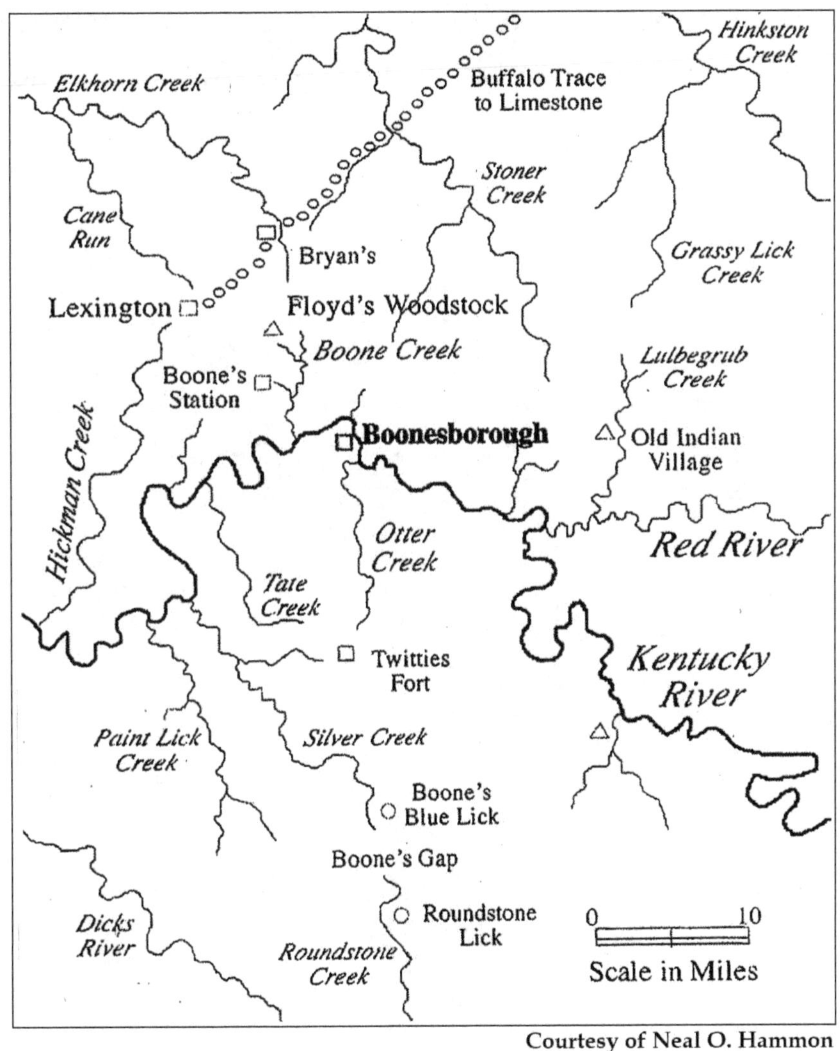

Courtesy of Neal O. Hammon

What the men were about to embark on was a journey born of curiosity. Their minds were probably racing: What is this place they call "Kentucke" that nobody has ever seen? What is over there, anyway? It is easy to imagine the affable John Finley, snatching his hat from off his head and urging his mount forward into the first step of the unknown. He had wanted to make this trip for fourteen years, ever since the Major General Braddock defeat.

4
Through the Gap and Beyond

"We proceeded successfully, and after a long and fatiguing journey through a mountainous wilderness, in a westward direction, on the seventh day of June following, we found ourselves on Red River. ..."—Colonel Daniel Boone

Those adventurers certainly knew from experience the discomforts, perils, and dangers they would face on their expedition. But that did not dampen their spirits. Little did they know that their journey and the sacrifices they would make would one day become an important part of Kentucky's history. The road they ultimately found through the wilderness would be one that hundreds of thousands of migrants would use on their way to a new home. Unfortunately, their present jubilation, however, would quickly turn to sorrow when one of them fell victim to the savage Indians soon after they had reached their Eden.

As the men left the Yadkin Valley, they entered wilderness that Daniel was already familiar with from his hunts near the Clinch and Holston Rivers and other parts of Virginia and Tennessee. The explorers had to be careful using these trails because of the threats to their safety from a few of the ever present Shawnee, Cherokee, and other Indian tribes.

The Indians had become more and more resentful of intrusions into their hunting grounds. In fact, they were regularly committing hostile acts, and even atrocities, against hunters they found on their territory who were wearing hunting gear or provisioned for permanent settlement. Daniel himself would soon suffer the devastating loss of his oldest son, who was tortured and killed by bloodthirsty savages.

Daniel seemed to seek danger and was usually around if there was any hint of trouble. He was always on the lookout for Indians who might be intent on doing him harm. He was well-suited for the venture; and, above all else, he was doing exactly what he loved to do. The other adventurers included experienced woodsmen, who would help divide the work more evenly and strengthen the defenses against potential Indian attacks.

John Finley was no stranger to the frontier. As a trader, he had already made his way deep into the Kentucky wilderness. Assaulted by Indians while trading in Kentucky, he showed no signs of fear and effectively dealt with the Indian situation. He was probably useful in lending encouragement to the others; he must have kept them entertained and in good humor as Irishmen are known to do. Daniel already knew that finding Cumberland Gap would require the crossing of high mountains, sometimes swollen streams, and other troublesome features of the landscape. He was aware that they needed to find their way to Powell Valley, which was girdled by the steep white cliffs of the Cumberland Mountain. Those cliffs would point the explorers to the Cumberland Gap.

The first night spent on the trip was uneventful. From all appearances, a compatible and able group had been assembled. At the time of the expedition, Daniel was already familiar with many of the networks of paths throughout the wilderness of Tennessee, North Carolina, Virginia, Kentucky, and other places, laid down through centuries by warring Indians, herds of bison, and hunters seeking game. Indians referred to them as Athawoninee, and hundreds of miles of such paths could be found east of the Mississippi River.

Without them, travel into the vast wilderness by immigrants would have been impossible without an army of axmen. It had taken centuries of movement to carve foot roads into the landscape, and they were used widely because they nearly always marked out the route of least resistance around mountains, streams, and other impediments to travel by foot.

A journey from the Yadkin Valley in North Carolina to Powell Valley and Cumberland Gap would intercept several such foot paths, thus reducing the time and distance of travel. Long hunters like Daniel became very familiar with the trails in the areas where they frequently hunted, and Daniel knew precisely which paths to take. On this particular journey, he would pass through several gaps in the Appalachian Mountains, including Moccasin Gap, Kane Gap, and most importantly, Cumberland Gap, which he had not seen during any of his hunts. Passage through that gap made it possible to penetrate the last of the great mountain barriers on their way to the interior of Kentucky.

The first white man who reported traveling through the Cumberland Gap was Gabriel Arthur. His captors, Shawnee Indians, led him through Cumberland Gap in 1674. More recently, Dr. Thomas Walker, credited with Cumberland Gap's discovery in the 1750s, had led a trek through the gap as an agent for the Loyal Land Company. Apparently, he did not take enough notice of the Warrior's Path; otherwise, he might have used it to get to the Blue Grass. Around the same time, a long hunter, Elisha Wallen, and his party roamed the area for more than a year-and-a-half, crossing the trail back and forth several times.

Daniel had remembered entering Kentucky, but he had made his entry into far eastern Kentucky, which turned out to be a catastrophe. In his 1767 hunt, he reached the Big Sandy River, but then had to turn back after encountering high mountains and a heavy snowstorm. Unknown to Daniel and John, entering Kentucky by way of Cumberland Gap would have other important things going for it—notably, the Cumberland River landscape, which immediately follows a water gap, the Narrows, and which is much more hospitable to a traveler going north.

In successfully reaching the Cumberland Gap, which was the first leg of their adventure, Daniel, John, and their fellow travelers probably crossed the north fork of the Holston River. They followed the familiar trail through Moccasin Gap and through Kane Gap down to Wallens Creek, crossing Powell River into the Powell Valley and on to Cumberland Gap. From there, they followed the clearly marked Warrior's Path to central Kentucky, stopping at a spot on the Red River where they established a station camp.

After entering the Powell Valley, Daniel's party was surprised to meet several men near what is now Rose Hill, Virginia. They were planting a crop of corn and building a settlement. This first attempt to settle was being made by the resourceful Joseph Martin. When completed, the Martin Station would prove to be the furthermost settlement on the western frontier. It was intended to be a convenient place for settlers who were migrating to Kentucky to provision themselves. Joseph had been contacted by Dr. Thomas Walker, agent for the Loyal Company, which owned most of the Powell Valley, about planting settlements in the valley in exchange for 21,000 acres of his choice.

Joseph chose the necessary land and built cabins at what is now Rose Hill, Virginia. However, as he was settling down in successful compliance with the terms of his agreement, a party of belligerent Indians arrived. One of the warriors seized Joseph's rifle; but, he quickly retrieved it. The Indians left in an angry mood, so Joseph and his party left for eastern Virginia. The Indians were doubtlessly angry that Joseph was building a permanent settlement at a time when they were at peace with the whites — on land that they hunted.

Joseph doubtlessly was familiar with the entire area through Cumberland Gap and directed Daniel's party on how to get there. That was not difficult to do; the Warrior's Path turned into Cumberland Gap only a short distance away. In exchange for directions, and perhaps provisions, Daniel and the other explorers may have helped Joseph's workers in their work.

The Cumberland Gap is an opening in the Cumberland Mountain that makes it possible to pass through it in a wagon or on a draft animal without having to climb a mountain. It actually presents itself as two openings in two mountains: one breaching the tall Cumberland Mountain and the other being a water gap located just thirteen miles distant at the crossing of modern-day U.S. Route 119 into Pineville. The first gap, called Cumberland Gap, or Cave Gap, has gotten all the glory while the lower gap, the Narrows, is largely overlooked except by a single historical marker near the entrance to Clear Creek in Bell County.

The connection between Cumberland Gap and the Warrior's Path to the exploration and settlement of Kentucky was in John Finley's mind at the inception of the explorers' venture. He had observed the Warrior's Path in his journeys into Kentucky as a trader and wondered if it did not extend south to an opening in the mountains that might furnish a way in and out as a north-south passageway.

It is surprising that Daniel, Benjamin, Thomas, Elisha, or any of the other adventurers had not already recognized that possibility in the early days after the discovery of Cumberland Gap. It is true that entry into Kentucky was stymied by the proclamations against development of western land; however, its discovery provided a catalyst for exploration and settlement by those undeterred souls who chose to ignore those edicts.

The ultimate benefit of this 1769 expedition to settlers and migrants was the creation of a wilderness road that went far beyond what either John or Daniel would have expected and what is with us today. The excitement caused by the discovery of the route from the Ohio River in the North to Cumberland Gap in the South by this expedition lives on in songs and poems written about it, national parks built around it, and the many books and papers published about it. Additionally, millions of public dollars have been spent in recent years to bring back Cumberland

Gap to its original glory through tunnels and restoring the gap's original contours.

5
On to Canaan

"Nature was here a series of wonders, and a fund of delight. Here she displayed her ingenuity and industry in a variety of flowers and fruits, beautifully colored, elegantly shaped, and charmingly flavored; and we were diverted with innumerable animals presenting themselves perpetually to our view."—Colonel Daniel Boone

It must have been a thrilling experience for John to finally realize that such a passageway really existed, and he knew what it meant to future settlers, looking for a southern entrance into Kentucky and a route to the Bluegrass. Having easily passed through Cumberland Gap, the explorers probably camped near the Yellow Creek on the Kentucky side, had a meal to celebrate the events of the day, and retraced their steps into the gap, pleased with their discovery.

The stately sandstone cliffs of the Cumberland Mountain facing the Powell Valley had been breached with no difficulty, and the explorers found themselves at the entrance of a new and unspoiled land. The limestone cliffs of the Cumberland Mountains overwhelmed the landscape, rising to heights of 1,645 feet, and they were almost in perpendicular formation. The warm May sun, the roar of cold water issuing in a torrent from the base of one of the mountains, and all the other sights and sounds lifted the men's spirits as they happily resumed their quest for the new Eden. For a moment, they felt the joy of discovery and were quite ready to move on.

The parties awakened to the morning after having spent their first night in Kentucky. They probably found intrepid Daniel missing from his blanket, scouting for directions and looking for evidence that the Indians might be nearby, watching their movements. If they wanted, they might have had breakfast of fresh rock bass fished from the stream, boiled duck eggs gathered from the river banks, and river mussels, all prepared over a blazing campfire. Later, they probably discussed yesterday's good fortune and listened to Daniel tell them what to expect to find on their first day in the wilderness. They would continue to follow the Warrior's Path, taking advantage of the pathway that the Indians had so conveniently provided.

After packing and leaving camp, they led their

horses about 13 miles north along the banks of the Yellow Creek to a place where that stream intersects the Cumberland River as it flows northwardly. Turning left a short distance, they heard the roar of turbulent rapids, or shoals, running through the water gap, which Dr. Walker had named the Narrows. The beginning of the shoals is now located downstream from the U.S. Route 119 bridge into Pineville. Further down, the shoals become much more shallow. The explorers were able to cross by foot or on horseback from this area. The crossing eventually became known as Cumberland Crossing, almost as familiar to the migrants as the two gaps.

At this time, there were no bridges in Kentucky to cross rivers and streams and few, if any, ferries to take the travelers across to dry land. The only way to get across these hurdles was to find a shallow place in the swift-flowing waters, take off one's moccasins, and carefully cross by foot. There was always the danger of drowning from the often-clumsy attempts at crossing, and there were few attempts at crossing that did not end with laughter and heckling by those who had made it across. Travelers would sometimes travel for miles through dense underbrush in search of a river crossing only to find that a heavy rain had swollen the river, making it impossible to cross by foot or on horseback. When that happened, the only thing left to do was to find another crossing or build a shelter and wait for the tide to go down, which often took several days.

The Narrows, which breach the Pine Mountain and lie approximately thirteen miles to the north of Cumberland Gap, were created over millions of years by the abrasive waters of the Cumberland River. In 1769, before the days of strip mining, clear-cutting of forests, and other forms of industrial development, streambeds, as a rule, were at or near bedrock with a scattering of large boulders too large and too heavy for the forces of the water to move them forward. The result was deeper rivers and rivers with greater force. In the case of the Narrows, the sides of the gap came close to the banks, narrowing the space through which the water must flow.

The sight of the whitewater combined with its sound was, at the same time, beautiful and awe inspiring. The Narrows, as seen today, are shallow, slow moving, and unimpressive. Both gaps are necessary to gain access to the Cumberland Valley, which lies in the direction of the Warrior's Path and runs northwardly toward the interior of Kentucky. If either gap was not there, the other gap would be useless for such purpose. A traveler would need to find another location before he or she could breach the Pine Mountain because the trail would become a dead end at Pineville.

Without the Cumberland Gap, a traveler would have to find a way to the headwaters of the Cumberland River and follow it through the Narrows thirty-three miles to the Cumberland Valley. That river was formed by the gathering of the waters of Poor Fork, the Martins Fork, the Clover Fork, and Catrons Creek in Harlan County at Baxter. It would be fortunate if there was some way to repair the Narrows and restore them to some approximation of their original glory.

A review of the topography contiguous to the Narrows makes it clear that the transportation facilities now in place can't be rerouted, and the landscape can't be reclaimed to its original beauty. But some day, the money might be found to do something to acknowledge its importance to the history of Kentucky and remind the public of this national treasure.

The Cumberland Valley, which initiates at the end of the Narrows and tends north is—when compared to much of the topography around the southern borders of Kentucky—relatively free of physical obstructions to travel by foot or horseback. Leaving the Narrows and traveling north, the explorers forded the old Cumberland Crossing, which was located approximately one-tenth of a mile downstream from Pine Street in Pineville, and at the place where the old Pine Street Bridge crossed the Cumberland River. This crossing served several hundred years of human history and was used by a quarter million immigrants on their way to a new life.

It is hard to pass through this historic complex of gaps and streams without imagining the young George Rogers Clark with his britches rolled up and his moccasins held high, negotiating the Cumberland Crossing on his way to Williamsburg, Virginia, from Harrodsburg, where he successfully implored the Revolutionary Convention to make Kentucky a county.

It is also easy to imagine Dr. Thomas Walker passing through the Cumberland Gap, through the Narrows, and across the Cumberland Crossing on his way to explore the countryside on behalf of the Loyal Company.

From the Cumberland Crossing, the party proceeded in a northerly direction until they reached Flat Lick. As its name implies, Flat Lick was a familiar place for animals to congregate to satisfy their need for salt and for travelers to refresh themselves and get some rest. Rumor has it that Daniel camped for a time at Stinking Creek, a few miles north, before crossing other creeks and ultimately reaching Robinson's Creek of Laurel River. The group then crossed Rockcastle River and proceeded up its west branch near its head where they set up camp.

After reaching the Rockcastle River, the party stayed put for a while, replenishing their supply of beef jerky and refreshing their horses. They also began to look for a good location to build a permanent camp. In organizing a hunt, one of the first items to be dealt with is the construction of a base camp. It is a place where members of the hunting party can camp, provisions can be stored for later use, and where hides and furs for the market can be kept. Daniel looked for a place near a salt lick where game gathered and where it would be easy to kill.

6
Land of Milk and Honey

"I had gained the summit of a commanding ridge, and, looking round with astonishing delight, beheld the ample plains, the beauteous tracts below."—Colonel Daniel Boone

Daniel set out alone to see what was ahead as was his custom. He ascended a high knob that gave him an unforgettable view of a vast wilderness filled with the flora and fauna of a perfect Eden. He must have been overwhelmed with the sights of forests, rivers and streams, green flowing meadows yielding slightly to the spring breezes, herds of buffalo, and hoards of other wild animals. He was probably the first white man to ever see it.

Daniel never claimed to be like Moses, but what happened on that knob sounds a lot like Deuteronomy, Chapter 34. Just before Moses died, the Lord showed him from the heights of Mount Nebo and Pisgah the vast lands that he had given the Hebrews, saying, "I will give it unto thy seed; I have caused thee to see it with thine eyes but thou shalt not go over thither." Ironically, Daniel, who was among the first settlers to view the splendor of Kentucky, and who saw it from many vistas, left the Commonwealth and died an aging old man without ever owning even an acre of it.

Daniel quickly returned to the explorers' camp and found John and the others waiting for his return. They were impatient to resume their journey and eager to locate and start construction of a base camp. Daniel told them what he had seen from the high eminence; he had seen every man's dream of the land of milk and honey — the so-called Promised Land. His enthusiasm must have caused shouting, backslapping, and maybe a little bit of the Irish jig. They resolved to retrace Daniel's steps so that they, too, could view the incredible Promised Land.

The travelers moved northwardly through inclement and uncomfortable weather. Daniel selected a spot for camp on a creek on Red River, which he named Station Camp Creek. More than likely, there was some haste to erect the shelters because of the threat of bad weather. The plenteous game they saw made the prospect of hunting for furs and skins more exciting. The base camp was erected while Daniel and his companions hunted.

John, not a professional woodsman himself, nevertheless started off alone to look for the old Indian town on Lulbegrud Creek where he had traded 14 years previously. The Warrior's Path in that vicinity ran along Station Camp Creek by the Indian town called Eskippakithiki and was easily found. John returned to the camp ten days later and reported that he had found the old town he had been looking for. Sadly, all the Indian dwellings had been set ablaze, but some of the timbers were still standing. He, Daniel, and John Stewart then set out to reach the town and found it where John said it would be.

Daniel and John Finley were not content with merely seeing Kentucky from the top of a knob. While the rest of the party hunted, they set out again, exploring the wilderness together. Unfortunately, John became ill, and he was unable to continue his trek with Daniel. Furthermore, he was unwilling to risk the hardship involved in such an exploration. It was more likely that John was having difficulty keeping up with Daniel because of his advancing age and fatigue. Daniel left him, alone, after first building him a basic shelter and leaving enough food to last him for ten days. It is hard to imagine John alone to face an untamed wilderness with hostile Indians, wild animals, and other dangers of the wilderness lurking nearby.

Daniel ascended another high summit and again saw the great pristine wilderness with awe and wonder. He would remember that scene fifteen years later when he related to John Filson that he "having thus proceeded along to the heights which overlook this terrestrial paradise, so descended into those fertile plains which are unequaled on our earth, and laid the fairest claim to the description of the garden of God."

John Finley, having recovered sufficiently, went out again with Daniel, and they more carefully explored what they had seen. Eventually, they returned to the base camp to describe to the others the wonders they had come across. Thus began a prolonged investigation into the game rich wilds of Kentucky, the likes of which Daniel had never seen before. All during that remaining summer and into December, each man was free to go his own way, but the men devoted most of their hunting to the taking of deer. Daniel, John Finley, and John Stewart often hunted and explored together.

Daniel added much to his growing knowledge of Kentucky's geography, which would serve him well in the coming years. He would slowly and methodically unlock the secrets of the land. His increasing familiarity with Kentucky became known to men like Richard Henderson, who later employed him in a grandiose scheme to buy the vast twenty million acres of Kentucky and Tennessee land from the Cherokee Indians, much of which Boone had explored.

Daniel, John Stewart, and John Finley hunted while the others stayed at the camp, preparing hides for sale. Daniel went far into the wilderness, going as far as the falls of the Ohio where Louisville would one day be built. He took pains to record the many salt springs and salt licks that he observed during that period. Additionally, he found gushing springs, caves, canebrakes, meadows, and all kinds of bison, deer, and turkey in their natural habitats.

Daniel, upon his return, located several additional places for camps and decided to disperse them over a wide area so as to provide more safety from marauding Indians and hungry animals. He made sure to have the smaller camps surround the main station camp while keeping them all at a safe distance from each other. Each camp was designed and equipped to store and protect the explorers' hides and furs before they were taken to market, as well as some of the provisions and supplies.

Those who remained at camp stayed busy preparing the deer skins for market. This was a tiring job as the men meticulously scraped the hair off the hides with a knife and conditioned each skin by running it across a board until it was soft and white. The process ultimately made the skins lighter and enabled them to pack more skins into a bundle.

Overall, the hunt proved to be a success. During the hunt, Squire Boone, Jr., Daniel's younger brother, fresh from the settlement, had supplied the men with ammunition, traps, and a fresh supply of salt that would later be paid for by the sale of the furs and skins from the hunt. It was planned that when the horses had been laden with skins and furs, Squire, Jr., would take them back to the Yadkin Valley, sell them, and then use the money to pay off debts and re-provision the hunt. Daniel was happy to have accumulated such good peltry, and he was even more thankful that they had not seen a single Indian while exploring Kentucky. However, things would soon change, and Daniel would find himself lamenting the loss of a son a year-and-a-half later.

Squire Boone, Jr., was ten years younger than Daniel, but he played a major role in Daniel's life. He was an excellent gunsmith and blacksmith, and the two young men went on several expeditions together. On the trip in 1769, which earned Daniel credit for the discovery of the Bluegrass area of Central Kentucky, Squire, Jr., was the person in charge of keeping Daniel supplied with ammunition and food provisions on his long hunts. Additionally, Squire, Jr., was right there when the Wilderness Trail was marked for the Henderson Company.

Squire, Jr., had a full and interesting life as a woodsman; in fact, it was a life that rivaled Daniel's. It has been reported that Squire, Jr., received eleven wounds during the Revolutionary War—a record number—and he suffered the effects of those wounds for the rest of his life.

On December 22, 1769, Daniel and some companions ventured into the wilderness again. They were unaware that a large party of Shawnee Indians was nearby, closely watching the explorers and waiting for an opportunity to capture them. As the explorers attempted to cross a low rise, the Indians, who had been concealed in a dense canebrake, suddenly rushed out and immediately took the unsuspecting men as prisoners.

The Indians had been on their way to their village on the other side of the Ohio River after a hunt on the Green River when they first noticed the explorers. The Shawnee leader, who went by the name of Captain Will, along with others in the party angrily demanded to be told where their furs and camps were. They also threatened to kill the explorers if they did not comply with their demands.

Daniel readily agreed to whatever the Indians wanted, knowing that the consequences of refusal might well be the tomahawk or scalping knife — or both. Always resourceful, Daniel decided that the best way to avoid death and the loss of property was to feign cooperation and good humor, and he craftily led the Indians to one of the outlying station camps where he and his companions had stored fewer furs, skins, and other property.

When the group reached the station camp, Daniel was glad to see that one of the camp keepers was there. At Daniel's instruction, the camp keeper quietly stole away, unnoticed. Daniel hoped that the camp keeper would give the other camps notice of their captivity so they could quickly hide their other furs and skins out of sight. However, he must have been very angry to find, when the group finally reached the main station camp, that nothing had been hidden. As it turned out, all of the camp keepers had quickly taken themselves out of harm's way, leaving the furs and skins exactly where they had been.

The Indians, having secured the booty, finally

permitted Daniel and his party to leave. Before letting them go, they gave the explorers each two pairs of moccasins, a deerskin, a small trading gun, and a small quantity of powder and shot to enable them to get food on their way back to their homes.

They also gave the men a warning: "Now, brothers, go home and stay there. Don't come here anymore. These parts are the Indians' private hunting grounds. All the animal skins and furs are ours. If you are so foolish to venture here again, you may be sure the wasps and yellow jackets will sting you again."

Some have insisted that the Indians were merciful, but Daniel was unable to see that the return of property for which they had worked so hard was a merciful act. Regardless of his feelings, though, he and his companions pretended to part on good terms.

It had required some time for the Indians to rob all of the various camps and to appropriate all of Daniel's possessions, and Daniel had to accompany them as they gathered the property from each camp, causing him unforgettable grief and pain. Eventually, the Indians set off for their villages north of the Ohio River, and John Finley, the camp keepers, and Daniel's other companions came out of hiding. Daniel, probably with a mix of sadness and anger etched into his face, insisted that everyone forget their decision that had already been announced to abandon the hunt and return to their families on the Yadkin. Instead, he suggested that they stay at the station camp while he and John Stewart went after the Indians to try and regain their possessions and a few horses. He hoped that they'd return to camp in two or three days.

With that, Daniel and John Stewart began their dangerous mission while Squire, Jr., and Alexander Neely, a seasoned hunter from the Yadkin Valley, remained at the station camp. After a time, the two men overtook the Indians and hid themselves under the cover of darkness. In the early morning hours, after patiently waiting for the best opportunity to keep from awakening the sleeping Indians, they found their horses nearby the camp and quietly led four or five of them away.

They kept up their flight throughout the coming day and night without slowing except to afford the horses some rest, food, and water. After enough time had gone by, Daniel and John were sure that the Indians had awakened, discovered the horses were gone, and went on their way toward the Ohio River.

When it was time to rest the horses again, Daniel suddenly heard the distant sound of fast-moving horses. When he looked up, he saw that several Indians were coming over the crest of a hill. He and John didn't have a chance to escape or try to hide themselves. In such circumstance, they had no choice but to surrender, and they smiled as much as they could to convey to the Indians that it was all a playful game.

Some of the Indians were angry and threatened injury; however, some of them appeared amused at the recapture of the prisoners and the horses. They expressed delight and ridicule by tying bells around Daniel's neck and causing the horses to strut around the campsite. After some time, the Indians then resumed their trip toward the Ohio River with their rich load of booty. They would enter their village armed with stories of how the dumb white men had thought they could escape and how easy it had been to recapture them.

In spite of Daniel's apparent acceptance of his incarceration, the Indians kept him and John under close observation. At night, the prisoners were stationed between two guards so that the guards would be able to detect any escape efforts. During the day, however, the Indians allowed them to roam freely around the campsite. Captain Will repeatedly assured the two men that the Indians intended to release them once they had crossed the Ohio River on the way to their villages.

After seven days of travel, and when they had

almost reached the banks of the Ohio River, the Indians made their camp. While they were working in various places—building fires, cutting wood, carrying water, and doing other chores—Daniel and John were able to communicate, through signs, a plan on how they would escape.

When the moment to escape finally presented itself, Daniel and John each grabbed a gun and ammunition, which had been carelessly left unattended by the Indians, and disappeared into thick cane that was growing near the campsite. Soon, they stealthily managed to put themselves just beyond the Indians' reach.

They remained under the thick cover and could hear the Indians making preparations to resume their trip. After enough time went by, the pair safely made their way toward the station camp. However, upon arrival, they saw that the camp had been abandoned. There was no sign of their companions. When they found evidence that the others had only recently left, they knew they needed to move quickly if they wanted to catch up with the others. Their assessment was correct, and they soon overtook their fleeing companions approximately fifty miles from the station camp.

Imagine Daniel's surprise and gratification to see that Squire, Jr., had joined the others and arrived with supplies to renew the hunt and expand the men's exploration. Also with Squire, Jr., was Alexander Neely, who had agreed to join Daniel and John Stewart in another assault on the Kentucky wilds. After what must have been a heated and contentious discussion, it was settled that Daniel, John Stewart, Alexander, and Squire, Jr., would remain in Kentucky while the others, including John Finley, would return to the North Carolina settlements. Daniel and his three companions would continue the hunt alone with the hope of procuring enough furs and skins to pay the large indebtedness that Daniel already owed — and which had grown substantially due to his younger brother's purchases. John Finley left the group, probably to return to Pennsylvania where his kindred lived, and the rest of that party turned toward the Yadkin.

The four remaining companions turned their direction toward the old Station Camp where they remained for a short time. After selection of a winter camp, they changed their hunting from deer to trapping for beaver and otter. Only a single camp was needed and less labor was required to prepare the pelts for sale since they were not as large or bulky. Additionally, the skins of the water animals brought a better price. Overall, trapping was far more lucrative than hunting deer, provided that the animals were sufficient in numbers.

Daniel and John divided the traps equally and agreed to hunt in different places. They would meet at the camp on designated days every two weeks. In order to reach all parts of the trapping waters, they constructed a canoe that would get them back and forth across the river. In 1770, in dead winter, John took the canoe out by himself and crossed the Kentucky River while Daniel remained where he was to trap on the opposite side.

As was often the case, the Kentucky River flooded during the winter months, exceeding its banks. Two weeks after John had set out in the canoe, Daniel returned to their camp, as planned, but John was not there. Once the Kentucky River went down and Daniel could finally cross to the other side, he found the remnants of a fire and John's name carved in the bark of a tree. Strangely, John was still nowhere to be found.

Realizing that something could be wrong, Daniel frantically searched up and down the banks of the river, but he found no sign of his good friend. It was unlike John to desert a hunt or ignore an agreement, and there were no signs of foul play that Daniel could see. Ultimately, he crossed the river again, probably feeling confused and deeply saddened by the strange and sudden loss of his friend. The mystery remained unresolved for several years.

Then one day, while a crew of axmen was working on Transylvania's Trail to Boonesboro, one of the crewmembers found a skeleton in the hollow of a large tree. A powder horn was lying nearby, bearing the initials 'J.S.', carved on it. The powder horn was later identified as belonging to John Stewart. Upon further inspection of the skeleton, it was discovered that there was a hole in the left arm—a bullet hole. After some consideration, Daniel theorized that John had been wounded by Indians and was able to conceal himself in the hollow tree, where he ultimately succumbed to his wounds.

After the unfortunate incident with John, Daniel and Squire, Jr., spent almost all of their time trapping, except for when they were building a more habitable cabin in preparation for the cold winter months. They were mindful to stay close together so that they would not get separated; they didn't want what happened to John to happen to either of them. With winter approaching quickly, they spent some time killing game for food, which was usually deer and turkey, preferring to avoid beaver and otter meat.

That winter proved to be a difficult one. Daniel and Squire, Jr.—now alone in the wilderness— were exposed daily to death by savages and wild beasts. The end of winter and the advent of spring again found Daniel and Squire well acclimated to the perils and dangers of the wilderness. They had experienced a good trapping season, but their ammunition was nearly exhausted.

It never occurred to Daniel that it was time to go home and spend a little time with Rebecca and his children. However, Squire, Jr., must have felt homesick and missed his own wife and kids. With that, he packed the horses with the last furs and prepared himself for the trip back home. On the first of May — the anniversary of their original departure from the Yadkin Valley — Squire, Jr., said goodbye to his older brother and returned to the Yadkin Valley to liquidate their debts and procure replacement provisions.

Daniel, now alone in the wilderness, became despondent and perhaps disillusioned with his circumstances. But he soon found his self-confidence again, and started making preparations to resume the hunt and continue his explorations.

There were probably several reasons why Daniel spent his winters in the Kentucky wilderness alone, placing traps for beaver and otter. Some people have speculated that he remained in Kentucky to put himself beyond the reach of the courts, his creditors, and debtors' prison. Others think Daniel remained in Kentucky because he was employed by Richard Henderson to find out what he could about the new land. Then there are folks who speculate that he found the wildlife to be so profuse, and the hunting so good, that he just couldn't bring himself to leave it. Profit from a good harvest of beaver and otter exceeded that from the taking of deer, which was the main summer crop.

During the winter months, after the trees and bushes had shed their leaves, Daniel was presented with a better opportunity to explore Kentucky. He had increased visibility of the landscape—all the way to the horizon—when viewed from the higher elevations. The view of the countryside taken from the ground provides little by way of sight distance. Daniel probably had learned more about the topography of Kentucky by exploring it at a time when the leaves were on the ground.

Again, Daniel's lack of ammunition gave him an opportunity to do more extensive exploration and discovery, including touring various places such as the Ohio River, the Falls of Louisville, Big Bone Lick, the Bluegrass, and the other places that were remote from the station camp. Nearing the advent of the spring season, however, Squire, Jr., returned to replenish Daniel's supply of ammunition, and Daniel set about to spend the next few months hunting.

In March 1771, Squire, Jr., returned to the camp with packhorses, and he and Daniel loaded furs and skins onto the packhorses' backs. The two brothers were going to head back to the Yadkin Valley. However, while camping near Powell Valley and roasting some meat, they were approached by a party of several Indians. Again, they suffered the loss of their furs, rifles, and horses, and they were left destitute after many months of sacrifice and hard labor. After that incident, Daniel finally returned home to the Yadkin Valley. It had been two years since he had seen Rebecca and his children.

Daniel's return to the Yadkin Valley from his historic 1769 Kentucky expedition left him disappointed, frustrated, and even more in debt. However, he had found Kentucky to be everything he had been told it was. He had hunted and trapped for two years, but nearly all of his labor and the labor of his companions had been stolen from him. Furthermore, he had lost one of his most valued companions, John Stweart, to marauding Indians.

After going to Kentucky, Daniel had seen herds of bison—sometimes 500 or more; and, the farther he traveled inland the more bison he saw; and, the wider and deeper the trenches were in which they lay down while wandering from place to place.

What a shame that this dull and harmless creature, content with little more than a few clumps of grass or a taste of salt, would be exterminated in the magnitude of thousands for tongues, humps, and hearts while its flesh would be left for the wolves and the vultures to devour. Books have been written about these magnificent beasts, lamenting their disappearance, including Ted Franklin Belue's book, *The Long Hunt: Death of the Buffalo East of the Mississippi.*

Daniel was astonished by the available game that yielded skins and furs of great value. He had seen virgin land as far as the eye could see, filled with canebrakes, rivers and streams, and fertile and untouched meadows that were just teaming with wildlife. He had seen the Eden that John Finley and others had told him about. But that was not all that he saw.

He saw heinous acts of maddened savages who seemed ever ready to cleave the skull and steal the furs and property of the white man. He had braved many cold winter nights in damp caves to escape the animals and ravages of winter. When Daniel finally chose to return to the Yadkin Valley, he had the complete knowledge of a whole new world, what it had to offer, and what it would take to possess it.

7
Powell Valley Massacre

"I sold my farm on the Yadkin, and what goods we could not carry with us; and on the twenty-fifth day of September, 1773, bade a farewell to our friends, and proceeded on our journey to Kentucke, in company with five families more, and forty men that joined us in Powel's Valley." — Colonel Daniel Boone

In March 1771, a complaint for debt was filed in Rowan County, North Carolina, in time to greet Daniel on his return from the Kentucky wilderness two months later. He was accused of hiding from the law in an effort to avoid his debts. That's not all that welcomed him.

Besides the mounting debts and court cases, Daniel found a more populated Yadkin Valley that pushed the game even farther west, leaving professional hunters barely able to make a living. That had become a recurrent problem — one that dogged Daniel and other professional hunters wherever they went. Instead of changing occupations and laying down roots in one place—as many fathers and husbands would have done—Daniel held tight to the life of a hunter. Meanwhile, Rebecca always seemed ready to follow him or wait patiently for his return.

Shortly after he returned to the Yadkin Valley, Daniel moved to East Tennessee to Sycamore Cove, a settlement organized by the Watauga Association on land leased from the Cherokees. Following that move, Daniel hunted in various places in Tennessee, but he could not forget what he had seen recently in the Land of Milk and Honey. His dreams of living in the new land were unrelenting, and he had resolved to permanently move to Kentucky—but this time with his family.

In 1772, Daniel and his frequent companion on long hunts, Benjamin Cutbirth, made another trip to Kentucky. That trip strengthened Daniel's dream to relocate and settle his family there. He knew that such a move could not be undertaken alone and would require a number of stalwarts to join in. He probably shared his plan with Benjamin and his other companions before he returned home. While in Kentucky, Daniel most likely selected a spot for a settlement on the Kentucky

River at Otter Creek near Clays Ferry. That site, deep in the Kentucky wilderness and hundreds of miles from civilization, was also probably better suited as a habitat for the wolves and other carnivorous animals that occupied it.

As Daniel and Benjamin made their way home from Kentucky, Daniel met up with Captain William Russell, probably at his home at Castlewood on the Clinch River. Captain Russell was a woodsman and well known frontiersman himself. He was also a man of means and influence. He had his eye on developments in Kentucky for some time and had positioned himself to make a great deal of money from Daniel's proposed venture if it proved to be successful.

The meeting with Captain Russell was probably not accidental and might even have been rehearsed. Daniel told the captain about his recent trip with Benjamin and other companions into the wilderness, and how he had met surveyors, land agents, and others while gathering information to be used in staking claims to preferred land.

Daniel told Captain Russell that it was just a matter of time before the best land would all be taken, and anybody who wanted to get in on the rush for land had better get moving. Captain Russell had military warrants, which would legally allow him to settle on Kentucky land. The Fincastle surveyors had been in Kentucky all summer long, making surveys for men with military warrants. Captain Russell, when he finally located the land authorized by his warrants, picked a site just outside of the present Lexington on what is now called the Russell Cave Pike. He might have chosen the same site had the party reached the Bluegrass in 1773. The following year, when Daniel selected a site for another client, he also chose the Lexington area on what is now Hickman Creek.

Captain Russell quickly agreed to join Daniel in a plan to establish a settlement in Kentucky. Captain Russell's home on the Clinch River was convenient as a location from which to launch such a venture and could serve as a staging place for the journey. Daniel must have been very happy to get such a substantial man to join him and to provide the money and essentials to undertake the venture.

Apparently, Daniel himself had no financial interest in the venture. He was hired to serve as a guide and to recruit migrants to unite in the settlement. The two men agreed that it was important to launch the expedition as soon as possible so that they might take full advantage of the undeveloped venue.

Daniel immediately set out to find people who

were willing to undertake the dangerous expedition. There was no shortage of takers, either because of Daniel's persistence or his powers of persuasion. He quickly recruited forty men in the vicinity of the Bryan Settlement to join them, as well as several other woodsmen who were experienced in wilderness survival.

It was agreed that most of those recruits would leave their families at home and come for them later when the conditions and circumstances of settlement were more favorable. Daniel also recruited several other men who were experienced in wilderness living to join with him in the settlement.

It was planned that the large Bryan contingent would meet up with Daniel's group in Powell Valley near Cumberland Gap at a certain time. They left the Yadkin Valley and other points to the weeping of family members and friends who feared they might not see their loved ones again. After all, other hearty adventurers had gone and never returned, like John Stewart, who was probably still on their minds.

When they reached the base of Walden Ridge, Daniel made camp and waited for the Bryan group from the Yadkin Valley to arrive. While on their way to the meeting point, Daniel's group faced a shortage of flour. He felt they should replenish their supply for the hard trip ahead. With that, he decided to send his 16 year old son, James, and two young brothers, John and Richard Mendinall, to Castlewood to get the needed flour and to advise Captain Russell of their whereabouts.

Soon after their arrival at Castlewood, Captain Russell loaded the flour and farm implements on horseback and sent the young men on their way back to Daniel. He himself remained long enough to transact some business, intending to leave in time to overtake them. Returning with the flour were five teenagers: Captain Russell's son Henry, 17; James, 16; two younger brothers, John and Richard; and, another youth named Drake—and an adult guide called Crabtree, who was probably leading the group. There were also two adult black slaves, Charles and Adam. The adventurous youngsters happily made their way along the Warrior's Path until dark with no thought of what might be before them.

Daniel kept by the camp at the foot of Walden Ridge near Powell Valley to await morning and the arrival of the flour. During that time, Daniel, known as a great storyteller, probably had a few tales to tell. Crabtree, leading the young group from Castlewood, also camped at the foot of Walden Ridge, not realizing that Daniel's party was only about three miles distant and could easily have been reached.

Let's pause for a moment to consider what this expedition presented by way of danger to those making such a long journey on crude Indian pathways. We should also consider what they would have faced had they reached their destination. The facts call into question the judgment of those who put the five youngsters and three adults—virtually unprotected—on a trail or pathway that was inhabited by angry Indians, armed with loaded rifles and ready to commit mayhem. We should also think about what arrangements had been made by Daniel and Captain Russell for the safety and survival of the new settlers who had surrendered themselves and their families to this hopeful venture once they arrived.

As with other possible Kentucky locations for new settlements, Otter Creek, located on the Kentucky River, was wilderness. It was manifestly unprepared and unsafe for anyone but the most seasoned woodsmen able to cope with the severest challenges offered by a wilderness environment. Although Otter Creek wasn't so thickly covered with trees and vegetation, it had no shelters against the weather. It also didn't have any ground cleared for corn or other crops, let alone any fortifications for protection against marauding Indians.

The settlers could only take with them a limited amount of food, and it would be more than a year before they could clear the ground in Kentucky for gardens and plant and harvest the crops. The large group would have to survive largely on game. Moreover, the journey would require them to travel many miles on narrow paths while being subject to attacks by hostile Indians who were ready to kill and scalp women and children. It didn't matter who they attacked; they were bitter over the plan to settle white people on their hunting grounds. The Warrior's Path of Kentucky was no place for anybody who wasn't prepared to defend themselves against such dangers.

Equally questionable was Daniel and Captain Russell's apparent lack of attention for the safety of the young travelers accompanying them and their failure to take measures to keep them out of harm's way. They knew that Indian renegades, who were angry with the settlers who were there to hypothecate their hunting grounds, were roaming the wilderness along the very same paths. They also knew that those savages were ready to commit such atrocities as a warning to would-be settlers against attempting to settle in their hunting space. The venture was hastily planned and carried out in an effort to reach Kentucky before others had a chance to claim and settle the good land first. Unfortunately, the two men didn't think about the dangers of what could happen to young and inexperienced travelers.

As the young campers slept, a group of Delaware Indians, Shawnees and Cherokees, suddenly raided the encampment from a contiguous forest. They were determined to avenge the encroachment upon their hunting grounds. What happened next was related by Charles, one of the slaves who had managed to hide during what turned out to be a slaughter of the unprotected youngsters. Angered by the large group of people usurping their hunting rights, the Indians began firing into the group, instantly killing the two Mendinall brothers. Crabtree and Drake were able to escape, but young James and Henry were crippled by gunfire, leaving them unable to escape. Adam, the other slave, managed to conceal himself in brush where he also witnessed what happened.

While a group of Indians began to steal the supplies and horses, one of the Indians began to cut and stab James and Henry, severely wounding the defenseless boys. Other Indians soon joined the fray, apparently inspired by the sight of blood as

James and Henry tried to protect themselves a-
gainst the savage blows with their bloody, muti-
lated hands. The assault became more violent, and
the Indians began torturing James and Henry by
pulling out their toenails and fingernails. The
brutality did not end with their pitiful pleas for
mercy. It got so bad that the young men finally
begged to be killed. James died while crying out
for his mother. The boys' bodies had been mutilat-
ed to serve as a warning to anyone who dared to
intrude upon their hunting grounds that they too
would suffer the same fate.

Daniel and Captain Russell woke unaware of
the tragedy that they were going to face that day.
The bodies of the young victims were soon discovered by one of Daniel's party, who had stolen
some supplies and was returning to the settlement.
He went to the forward camp and warned them a-
bout what he had seen. Daniel immediately started
to build a rude fort to protect the frightened travelers and assigned Squire, Jr., to go to the campsite
and bury the victims.

The five boys were buried in a common grave
that was covered with logs and rocks to protect
them from hungry scavengers. Charles and Adam,
who had hid in the woods for several days, finally
returned to tell the group the awful story of torture

and barbarity. [Some twenty years later, Drake's bones were found near the area where the boys had been attacked.]

Squire, Jr., returned to the forward camp shortly after he had finished the burial and asked what the group should do next. Daniel, ever stoic, urged everyone to continue with the journey. At that point, however, the other immigrants were so frightened and disheartened that they quit the venture and returned to their homes. Rather than return to the Yadkin Valley, Daniel accepted an offer to use a cabin on the farm of Captain David Gass, located a few miles below his cabin at Castlewood, south of Clinch River, hoping to see a resumption of the settlement expedition.

Those acts of depravity were committed at a time when some of the Indians and whites were under a peace treaty, which may have been the reason why Daniel and Captain Russell had relaxed their vigilance and failed to provide more protection for the young travelers. The perpetrators were eventually identified, tracked down, and their leaders were executed. They included two Cherokee chiefs and some Shawnees.

It became apparent that the relations between the Indians and the settlers would soon provoke a war between those belligerents. Anticipating hostilities, Governor Dunmore, based on recommendations of Captain Russell, directed Daniel and Michael Stoner, one of Daniel's lifelong friends, to warn surveyor parties about an impending war. He also advised them to pack up their hatchets and surveying instruments and retreat to safety in the settlements. The two carried out their assignment with dispatch and received expressions of gratitude for their success.

8
Sold!

"I, being relieved from my post, was solicited by a number of North Carolina gentlemen who were about purchasing the lands lying on the South side of Kentucke River from the Cherokee Indians, to attend their treaty at Wataga, in March, 1775, to negotiate with them and mention the boundaries of the Purchase." —Colonel Daniel Boone

The murders of young James and Henry were part of a gathering storm of hatred and hostility between Indians and whites that signaled trouble for the border settlers of Kentucky and Tennessee. As settlements on Indian hunting grounds increased, so did the number of hostile acts by Indians, giving rise to apprehensions and retaliatory responses by whites. After almost a year of fighting in what became known as Dunmore's War, the Indians surrendered, effectively ending the war, and the settlements slowly returned to peace.

Anger arising from the murders in Powell Valley was widely credited with starting that war, but the murder of the family of Logan, a powerful Mingo chief in May 1774, was of equal or greater importance. A group of Virginia frontiersmen, led by Daniel Greathouse, ruthlessly murdered Logan's brother and other close relatives; one woman had been pregnant and was caring for her infant daughter. The Mingos had been living at the mouth of Yellow Creek on the Ohio when the frontiersmen lured them from their village to the cabin of a rum trader and murdered.

The savagery of the act is unparalleled. It shows that acts of barbarity were not confined to Indian deprecations against whites and that similar acts by whites against Indians were commonplace. Logan had enjoyed good relations with neighboring white settlers. He was not a war chief by any means. In fact, he was a village leader, respected by both the whites and the Indians. The murder of Logan's family represents one of the saddest events in Indian history and is recorded in the painful lament made by him following Dunmore's War:

"Colonel Cresap, the last spring, in cold blood and unprovoked, murdered all the relatives of Logan, not sparing even my women and children. There runs not a drop of my blood in the veins of any living creature. This called on me for revenge. I have sought it. I have killed many. I have fully flutted my vengeance. For my country, I rejoice at the beams of peace; but, do not harbor the thought that mine is the joy of fear. Logan never felt fear. He will not turn on his own heel to save his life. Who is there to mourn for Logan? Not one."—Logan

Word of Kentucky's rich interior was increasingly finding its way among hungry land speculators. Throughout 1774, surveyors were everywhere, marking trees with their hatchets, locating stakes, and recording the locations of natural monuments. The good land was being claimed quickly, and there was talk of opening Kentucky to claims by veterans of the French and Indian War. Ambitious men, like Captain Russell, who were ever on the lookout for a good deal, were casting their eyes upon all that free land and wondering what they could do to take advantage of the opportunities it presented.

Although Daniel's first attempt to establish a

permanent colony had failed, that didn't chill the land fever of enterprisers like Richard Henderson, who had visions of a colony governed by him and his investors under a feudal regime. Richard had hired Daniel. He was an opportunistic man and one of influence who, over the years, had conceived a grandiose plan to "buy" millions of acres of virgin land in Kentucky and Tennessee from the Cherokee Indians. Richard had considered organizing a land company of investors with principals in Rowan County, North Carolina, to raise money to purchase the land, but the scheme had progressed no further.

Richard was rich, influential, and ambitious. When Daniel made his successful foray into Kentucky in 1769, Richard was 34 and had served on both the local and appellate courts in North Carolina. Five years earlier, he had organized an investment company for the purpose of exploring investment opportunities and to profit in investments to the west.

To carry out his idea, there were serious obstacles he knew he must overcome. He must first establish that the Cherokee tribe was the owner of the land and that its ownership gave it the right, under prevailing law, to sell the land to a private land company. Moreover, what lay beyond the mountain to the west was still a matter of rumor and conjecture; and, he needed to find out what land was arable and where that land was located.

There were no topographical maps showing the elevations of the mountains and physical features of the landscape. There were no hydrological studies identifying the locations of waterways and other such information. There were no soil samples assessing the fertility and depth of soil for agriculture. Richard did not have available to him surveying crews, like the Loyal Company, to survey and plat the property and divide it into smaller tracts.

But he also was no fool. Experienced in the art of alternative thinking, Richard knew how to improvise a solution to those problems. He knew a young woodsman in Rowan County who had spent most of his years in the wilderness on hunting expeditions. The woodsman knew more about Kentucky than any white man alive.

Richard's plan was to purchase approximately twenty million acres of land lying to the west from the Cherokee Indians. On January 6, 1775, his business, Henderson Company, succeeded to Louisa Company, which had been already formed by him. So began a battle for the conquest and settlement of that huge tract of Kentucky wilderness, which included most of Kentucky and a large part of Tennessee. The plan called for the creation of a four-teenth American colony to be named Transylvania and governed by the company's owners as pro-prietors. This was based in part on the English feudal system and required assessment of the annual quitrent for each of the four hundred acres sold. Such quitrent was already being assessed and paid on other lands, but the proceeds were apparently under the control of the king.

Richard's plans were audacious to an extreme. As a lawyer and appellate judge, he was likely familiar with the Royal Proclamation of 1763, which prohibited such transactions. Land companies that had spent large sums of money exploring Kentucky, conducting surveys, and staking claims could find themselves with claims that were inferior to Transylvania's claim of ownership under the Cherokee deed. If such a conveyance could withstand the many criticisms leveled against it, Richard would pull off the greatest land deal in the history of conveyances. Transylvania's purchase was made during times of great confusion over ownership of unoccupied lands and the right of immigrants to acquire those lands. Had he found a way to buy a vast wilderness on the cheap and sucker expectant colonial officials in the process?

It was probably in early 1775 when Richard decided to make his big move. We do not know exactly what kind of relationship he had with Daniel prior to that date. However, we do know that there is evidence of frequent contact between the two men and mention of his name in correspondence between their investors. Daniel probably kept Richard's interest alive in the western land and the beauty that he had so graphically described.

It is possible that Daniel was being paid to explore Kentucky and to keep Richard advised of other developers who might also be interested in exploiting it. Or perhaps, Daniel was exploring in order to locate the best lands for acquisition. The reason why he remained in Kentucky through the uncomfortable winter months while his companions were returning home to be with their families might have been for such a purpose.

Richard and Nathaniel Harp soon traveled to several of the Cherokee towns where they persuaded the Indian leaders to sell their interest in Kentucky hunting grounds for what amounted to a few wagonloads of gaudy goods. The land to be conveyed included the land between the Kentucky River and the Cumberland River's mouth to the Ohio.

The Indians and Richard agreed to meet in

March at Sycamore Shoals on the Watauga River to negotiate and finalize the terms of the sale. Among the Indians supporting the sale was the influential chief, Atta Kulla Kulla, who was also known as Little Carpenter. He, along with several other tribesmen, traveled with Richard to North Carolina to inspect the goods to be provided as consideration for the sale. After some haggling, the Indian delegation selected the goods to be exchanged for land.

Even as Richard's plan for acquiring the Cherokee land was underway, ambitious men of every stripe were pouring into Kentucky from all directions, ignoring the grumblings of the governors of Virginia and North Carolina against buying or settling on Kentucky land. Avid settlers had migrated to Kentucky, staked claims to property, cleared land, and planted crops. The Cherokees' claim to that land was considered marginal. It was claimed that the Cherokees did most, if not all, of their hunting in locations other than in Kentucky; therefore, they had no preemptive rights to that land upon which they might hunt.

Land companies, private investors, and even the governors of the colonies of Virginia, North Carolina, and Pennsylvania were thunderstruck when news of the purchase was disseminated by

Richard that Kentucky was up for sale. If the sale went through, surveys and plats of Kentucky lands jamming some of their desks may soon be worthless and subject to the ownership of a Rowan County lawyer who didn't have a survey to his name. Richard had suddenly become the man of the hour and the man to be reckoned with. George Washington, the future father of that country, said of the transaction: "There is something in that affair which I neither understand nor like and wish I may not have cause to dislike it worse as the mystery unfolds."

Soon after, Richard hired Daniel to go into the villages and towns of the Cherokees to advertise that there would be a treaty with some white men at Sycamore Shoals in March to further discuss the proposal and ratify an agreement to finally sell Kentucky lands to the Transylvania Company. Daniel was also engaged to open a passageway from Long Island in the vicinity of the Holston River through Cumberland Gap and into the interior of Kentucky over Boone Trace, which later became the Wilderness Road. The passage had to be wide enough to handle packhorses and pedestrians, and it needed to be clearly marked. Richard felt that an established route would make it easier to recruit settlers who might purchase property.

Additionally, it would make them feel more secure in the exercise of that ownership.

As planned, the meeting between the Cherokees and representatives of the Transylvania Company occurred at Sycamore Shoals in early March 1774. A large number of Cherokees—possibly as many as twelve hundred—attended the meeting to witness the sale of the land and to collect their portion of the goods on display. At the proceedings, a carnival atmosphere prevailed, replete with the kinds of ceremonies that the Indians liked. There was food, entertainment, and even liquor, which was held in reserve until the Indians were ready to go home. The food was prepared by women who resided in the nearby Watauga community, a settlement located on lands leased from the Cherokees. It was a carefully planned program that had been thoughtfully organized by Richard and designed to eliminate any obstacle that might arise to the consummation of the transaction.

However, Richard was surprised when the discussion of the proposed treaty was met with strong opposition from Atta Kulla Kulla's son, the young Chief Dragging Canoe. He and several other recalcitrant chiefs strongly objected to the sale, eloquently complaining that the transaction was just another step toward loss of all of their hunting grounds. Still, the Indians assembled were so tantalized by the display of goods that were laid before them that the chiefs were made to submit to the transaction by Indians determined to get their part of the treasure.

Richard had intentionally laid out the goods in a place where the expectant Cherokees could see them, and his ploy produced the desired result in the end. One observer estimated that the goods were estimated to be valued at ten thousand pounds sterling. Others, however, gave a substantially lower value. The deed conveying the property recited a consideration of only 2,000 pounds sterling, which is presumed to be the correct price paid.

After the ceremony concluded and the deed was ultimately signed, there arose a complaint by some Cherokees that the goods were of low quality; the Indian leaders who executed the agreement and chose the goods had let the Indians down. Dragging Canoe must have been the ultimate hero of the tribe because of his opposition to the sale. He later became the leader of a group of Indians who were violently opposed to any homesteading by the white man on their hunting grounds.

The deed was executed on March 17, 1775, but Daniel was not there for the signing. He had already left for Long Island, near what is now Kingsport, Tennessee, where Benjamin Cutbirth and 29 other sturdy axmen had gathered. Richard was wasting no time. He knew that he would be able to establish a settlement in Kentucky and blunt the mounting opposition to his ownership only if he could provide access to the property—and soon.

Unfortunately, there was no time to build a roadway that was wide enough to accommodate wagons. However, there was already such a road between what is now Kingsport and Martin Station near the Cumberland Gap that was wide enough for wagons. The plan was to provide a passageway of sufficient width to accommodate packhorses and farm animals with the idea of building a better road as the land was sold and the project progressed. In building this roadway, Daniel would establish a route that would, in time, become the major route in and out of Kentucky. It would also serve hundreds of thousands of migrants who were entering and leaving Kentucky. That road became known as the Wilderness Road.

As Daniel was leaving for Long Island, Atta Kulla Kulla turned to him and said, "We have given you a fine land, but I believe you will have much trouble in settling it." That prophecy would become a reality. As it t urned out, Richard's purchase was a foolish and almost childish gamble. But it did not cost him very much to get his deed to Kentucky beyond a few wagonloads of gaudy trinkets. Holding onto ownership would be another matter, and one that would consume a lot of investors' money over the next several months.

This might be a good time to reflect on the sale of Kentucky and consider the fairness of the transaction to the assembled Indians. The Indians were popularly referred to as savages. They were uneducated children of the wilderness, living under the crudest of circumstances and dependent on nature for their daily venison. Simple things like blankets, shirts, and other cheap goods tantalized them, like schoolchildren. They were about to sell a part of what might be their hunting grounds for nearly nothing.

On the other hand, Richard was a lawyer, judge, and wealthy businessman with great persuasive powers as evidenced by his conduct during the treaty meeting. He was articulate, confident, and cunning. He had wagons full of cheap trading goods that he used to tempt the poor aborigines and keep them focused—or perhaps, distracted.

Another aspect of the sale to consider is any difference in value between the twenty million acres of untouched land that Richard got and the collection of baubles, trinkets, cheap trade rifles, and other random cheap goods paid to the Indians for their hunting grounds. Using Richard's own offer made a few months later to sell to the public four hundred acres at one pound sterling per one hundred acres (or four pounds sterling per four hundred-acre tract), the value would be two hundred thousand pounds sterling. That value does not take into consideration what the twenty million acres would be valued at if the price increased to ten pounds sterling per one hundred acres. The value of the property would then soar to as much as two million pounds sterling.

Considering the relative sophistication of Richard against the intelligence of the Indians, together with the difference in the amount received by each party, it would appear at first blush that Dragging Canoe was right; the Indians had been duped, getting by far the worst end of the deal. However, there are those who still disagree, contending that the Cherokees got paid for land they never even technically owned.

9

Henderson's Folly

"I soon began this work, having collected a number of enterprising men, well armed. We proceeded with a possible expedition until we came within fifteen miles of where Boonsborough now stands, and where we were fired upon by a party of Indians that killed two, and wounded two of our number; yet, although surprised and taken at a disadvantage, we stood our ground." —Colonel Daniel Boone

Richard Henderson's grandiose scheme to buy Kentucky on the cheap resulted in disappointment and loss to those who helped him. Daniel would lose his dream of Shangri La; Richard would lose his fourteenth colony and his dreams of power and riches; the Indians would lose their land; and, men and families would lose their homes. In some cases, men would also lose their lives.

Consider how potentially important this assemblage of obscure North Carolinians was to the future of Kentucky and all of America in the years to come. Robert Morgan, in his book, *Boone: A Biography*, describes the importance of an occupied Kentucky:

"It is easy to forget in the twenty-first century the significance for the English-speaking eastern communities of the settling and holding of Kentucky. The Bluegrass region was valuable in itself, almost beyond description, as a place to claim and build farms and towns and future cities and great wealth. Explorers and speculators and leaders of the time understood that a foothold in Kentucky served as a buffer against the Indians, against the British to the north, and perhaps the Spanish to the west and south. But even more than that, a settled Kentucky promised to open the whole Ohio Valley to settlement.

"… Whatever lay beyond, in the sunlit pastures and hills of coming years, Kentucky was the key, the first West, Kentucky was the threshold, the beachhead, to who-knew-what playlands and empires of the future, farther west."

Daniel's party of axmen started their work as road makers under a promise of approximately ten English pounds for a month of work, or enough to buy 540 acres of Henderson land. Daniel was to receive two thousand acres of land in the recently acquired Cherokee tract. Some of the workers who signed on for the work included David Gass, who had furnished Daniel and his family a cabin after he had failed in his first attempt to settle in Kentucky; Michael Stoner and Benjamin Cutbirth, frequent friends and companions on many hunting expeditions; William Hays, his son-in-law; and, William Twitty, Felix Walker, and others whose names and work are commemorated on a granite monument at historic Boonesborough in Madison County, Kentucky, home of Kentucky's first permanent settlement.

The work was exhausting and required the almost constant use of axes and other cutting tools. The workdays sometimes lasted from dawn and until sundown. The roadwork started several days before the departure of the trailing group of settlers, which included Richard Henderson. He was scheduled to arrive several days after Daniel's group, carrying most of the tools and other implements needed to establish the settlement and camp with a large supply of provisions.

It was thought that the journey would be free of attacks from Indian warriors. After all, Richard was on the land the Indians had just conveyed to him; there seemed to be no reason to post guards. The work involved widening and making clearly visible a narrow passageway by cutting bushes, falling trees, grubbing stumps, moving rocks, cutting canebrakes, removing other obstacles, and using already established and visible buffalo traces and pathways laid down by Indians and other animals whenever possible. Accompanying the road makers were Daniel's feisty 16 old daughter, Suzanna, and a slave, both of whom helped as camp workers. Daniel took a forward position where he could watch out for animals and Indians and kill any game that he might encounter.

Richard's party of settlers followed Daniel's axemen by as much as one hundred miles. He had been delayed by having to change loads from wagons to the backs of the horses to be transported to their destination. It became clear at the outset that Richard's attempt at settlement was better planned, better funded, better protected, and better provisioned in all aspects of wilderness travel and settlement than Daniel's attempt in 1769 when he lost his son, James, to Indian brutality. But that didn't mean that the migrants were not at risk.

Fourteen days into the road making, Daniel stopped to camp approximately 15 miles from Otter Creek, their final destination. His group failed to post a sentry to guard against any attacks by Indians for the reasons already stated. During the night, they were awakened from their sleep by rifle fire directed at their camp. Two of the axemen, Felix and William, were badly wounded, and William's slave fell into the campfire. The other men quickly grabbed their rifles and ran into the forest. Felix was also able to flee to safety. William was saved by his bulldog, which seized one of the Indians by his throat and threw him to the ground. Unfortunately, another Indian killed the poor dog, inflicting a fatal blow to the animal with his tomahawk.

Daniel nursed Felix, who sustained gunshot wounds to both knees, back to health by skillfully applying his knowledge of wilderness medicine to his companion's wounds. Felix, in a narrative written several years later, praised Daniel with expressions of gratitude for the tender care that he gave him on his return to health. William, however, soon died of his wounds. At another campsite, another Indian attack followed; two men were killed that time. Those raids caused great panic among the migrants, several of whom immediately returned to the settlements.

It was just the migrants who were afraid. Those savage acts provoked general fear and alarm throughout the expedition, causing a sizeable number of settlers to return to their homes. As Richard made his way toward Otter Creek on the newly established passageway, he was daily confronted with people fleeing Kentucky from other locations apart from Otter Creek. The exodus of settlers from this and other expeditions grew in numbers, and Richard feared that the venture was about to collapse.

Daniel quickly sent a letter to Richard, expressing alarm and cautioning him that he must join him as soon as possible if he hoped to save the expedition. After receiving Daniel's letter, Richard hastily engaged one of his groups to travel to Otter Creek to inform Daniel and the others that he was indeed on his way with reenforcements of men and provisions. He would endeavor to reach them as soon as he could. The returning messenger arrived safely at Daniel's camp with a promise from Richard of ten thousand acres of prime Henderson land for delivering the message.

Richard arrived at Otter Creek just in time to calm the frightened settlers who were traveling with Daniel. Felix required time to recover and recuperate, but that did not keep Daniel from marshalling his men and putting them to work, making ready the land where the fortress would be located. It was now time for him and the rest of the party to do what they came to do.

Having arrived at the designated site on the Kentucky River, Daniel began constructing shelters for his group and the rest of the party. Richard was first concerned with building a fortress that would be strong enough to repel assaults by marauding Indians and hungry predators to which the settlers might flee in the event of an attack. That priority alone showed his concern for the safety of his settlers. However, he soon found that he had problems that made it difficult to build a fort and to complete any project that he attempted to undertake himself. He realized that he needed to depend on Daniel for so many things, and he doubtlessly began to worry.

What if Boone suddenly quit the project and returned to the Yadkin Valley? Who among the settlement party could take on his responsibility? Who else commanded the respect for Daniel and his leadership? The expedition would surely fail. But he didn't need to worry; that was not in Daniel's nature. Besides, Daniel had dreamed for years of the time when he could start fresh with his family in Kentucky, and he was not about to surrender to such difficulties. If the project suddenly failed and everyone else went home, he would be the last to leave.

Other problems began to emerge, though, which impeded and endangered the expedition. Many of the settlers were either unwilling or unable to participate in the work needed to be performed for the common good. Many of them spent their time scouting the land or arguing over location of town lots or farming tracts that were being assigned to them. Of particular concern to Daniel and Richard was the wanton slaughter of valuable game, using the animals for target practice.

Sometimes the newcomers would kill three or four of the dwindling number of bison, cut out their tongues, remove the fillets from the creatures' humps, cut out their tasty livers, and then leave the carcasses for wolves and other predators to feast upon. They must have known by engaging in such sport that they were depriving the other settlers of needed food, which might someday even come off of their own tables.

A good number of settlers showed no interest in clearing the sites where the fortress was to be erected. They didn't want to work on the stockade or blockhouses to be erected at each corner of the fort, which were necessary in the defense of the fort. Rather, they spent their time clearing out their own garden spots, moping around the compound, napping, or showing other evidence of just being lazy. Added to these problems was the almost unanimous opposition to the transaction by men of wealth and prominence. In time, it became more certain that the venture undertaken by Richard would fail, and the scheme for the establishment of a fourteenth colony was not going to succeed. Eventually, Virginia nullified it through legislation.

10
That's Daddy

"On the fourteenth day of July, 1776, two of Col. Calaway's daughters, and one of mine, were taken prisoners near the fort. I immediately pursued the Indians, with only eight men, and on the sixteenth overtook them, killed two of the party, and recovered the girls." —Colonel Daniel Boone

In 1776, the colonies had declared their independence and were waging a war of separation from the mother country. The year was proving to be a busy one. Henderson and Company had been locked in a battle with Virginia, North Carolina, and just about everybody else disputing ownership of Kentucky. A petition to the Virginia Legislature would request the formation and adoption of a separate government for Kentucky. That request was being advocated by the young intrepid George Rogers Clark primarily for the purpose of shutting down Richard Henderson's goal for a feudal regime with him and his investors as proprietary rulers.

We have already shown that Richard's plan for a settlement at Fort Boonesborough was near failure because of the indolence and malaise of many of the immigrants he had shepherded onto the new land. A lot of the settlers had surrendered to disillusionment, disappointment, and fear of marauding Indians. However, several stalwarts remained at Fort Boonesborough, including the Boone family. It seemed that the only hope for survival of the expedition rested with Daniel, who seemed to always know what needed to be done—and how to do it.

Rebecca and the young children followed Daniel into their new life in the vast wilderness without complaint. Rebecca resumed the mindless work that she had done throughout her life as the wife of a wanderer and mother of so many children. Meanwhile, Daniel was concerned about the many problems confronting Richard's efforts to settle Kentucky, but he was determined to stay no matter what difficulties arose. Daniel had finally found his place in the sun, and he would not give it up easily.

There are no historical records of the routine activities that went on in Boonesborough, and so we must speculate what happened on the Sunday in July 1776 when Indians kidnapped three children from the settlement. Apparently, it had started out as a beautiful and peaceful morning. The settlers living at Fort Boonesborough hadn't encountered any Indian problems for several weeks. That afternoon, Daniel had been resting in his cabin, probably thinking about the next day's work and planning how he would get everything done. He was unaware that five Indians had been stalking Fort Boonesborough for several days, angered by its unwelcome improvements.

Some of the Boonesborough immigrants probably stayed busy doing chores or resting, as Daniel had been doing, for the next day's work, especially in the hot July sun. Children from different families might have been running around the cabins—singing, laughing, playing games, and enjoying the afternoon as kids have always been known to do. The older boys probably occasionally stopped their play to hurl stones from their slingshots at unwary rabbits or groundhogs. Other more ambitious men and women might have braved the hot afternoon sun, coaxing sprouts out of the black fertile soil.

Men and boys were gathered in small groups at various places; perhaps, they were looking forward to the evening meal. Some of the immigrants were usually nearby the Kentucky River, which at that point was wide, deep, and sometimes treacherous due to the swiftness of the water and the steep banks that girdled the stream. It was their Sabbath, and it was customary for the women and girls, if they were not busy helping with the evening meal, to put on their best finery. Men were more relaxed during this time.

Betsy Calloway's fiancé was busy shaving, while Nathan Reid and his friend, John Floyd, were strolling around the compound, enjoying the landscape. Rebecca and wives of the other men were probably fixing the night's supper in the shanty kitchen cabin. Supper may have consisted of slices of roasted bear meat, venison, and polk salad or other greens. Things at Boonesborough appeared to be normal.

But out on the Kentucky River, there developed a situation that alarmed both the Boone family and the entire Fort Boonesborough settlement. To this day, the incident is one of the most discussed and romanticized occurrences in Daniel's life as a woodsman. It is is verified by letters, oral testimonies, and manuscripts that were collected by Lyman Draper over a long period of time in an obvious effort to verify the story. Furthermore, it has remained mostly consistent since the early days when Colonel Floyd, a participant in the rescue, gave his account of what had happened.

Three young teenage girls—Jemima Boone, Elizabeth Calloway, and Frances Calloway—were trying to steer a canoe away from the steep north bank of the Kentucky River where the current had taken them. As the girls neared the bank, trying hard to avoid it, a group of Indians suddenly appeared from behind a curtain of brush, jumped in the water where it was shallower, grabbed the buffalo strap attached to the canoe, and began pulling it toward the north shore. Jemima and one of the Calloway girls, screaming at the top of their lungs, began hitting one of the Indians on his plaited head with their paddles with such vigor that both paddles broke in half.

Hearing all the commotion, Daniel grabbed his britches, pulled them on as fast as he could, and ran to the riverbank, wringing his hands in fear and anger. He hollered out for help as he ran toward the river. He was so frantic that he even forgot he was not wearing his moccasins. Richard Calloway, Elizabeth and Frances, grabbed his gun and joined the yelling crowd, loading the gun as he ran. By the time the crowd finally reached the water, the floating canoe, which was the only transportation to the other riverbank, was found empty and floating downstream, out of reach.

Richard and nine or ten other men from the fort quickly mounted horses and started for a shallow place in the river about a mile downstream, which they easily forded. Except for those few riders, the rest of the men and women just stood there, helpless to do anything. As for the canoe, someone had to swim to the other shore and retrieve it since there was no other transportation. That duty fell to twelve-year-old John Gass, who voluntarily jumped into the river and returned soon after with the canoe in tow. Once ashore, Daniel and five others immediately squeezed into the canoe, returned to the north shore, and ascended the riverbank where Daniel ordered his party to take different directions with hopes of locating the girls and their captors as fast as possible.

By that time, Richard's mounted party had already found the trail. He insisted that they follow that trail, but Daniel objected, explaining that should they suddenly come upon the kidnappers, there was a danger the girls might get killed. Daniel took charge of the rescue effort, and the eight rescuers decided to follow his lead because of his reputation. It was agreed upon that Richard and his horsemen would follow the trail that led to the lower Blue Lick. They hoped they could intercept the Indians at Licking Crossing. Daniel and his party would trail in the same general direction, but more cautiously.

The rescuers had pursued the Indians a distance of approximately five miles, and it was beginning to get dark. That's when they selected young John Gass to perform yet another heroic deed. He was dispatched from the campsite back to the fort to retrieve Daniel's moccasins, ammunition, provisions, and other articles of clothing. After safely reaching the fort and securing those items, John made his way back to the campsite alone, and he managed to reach it before daylight—a surprising feat for a 12 year-old boy. That evening, the Boone and Calloway parties came up with a strategy to try and save the three girls before it was too late.

At morning's light, Daniel and his party, accompanied by three experienced woodsmen whom they had happened upon that night, resumed their pursuit. They soon discovered the place where the Indians had camped the previous night. However, as they continued along, their tracking of the Indians became more difficult as a result of the Indians' efforts to conceal their movements.

Daniel understood the gravity of the situation, the high stakes involved, and the importance of correctly and speedily assessing the Indians' movements, and where they might be found. After much difficulty, the rescuers were able to correctly identify the trail. Daniel was sure that the Indians were headed for a Shawnee town located on the

Scioto River, and he felt that it would be unwise to pursue that route until the Indians relaxed and felt safer in their flight. Besides, Indians usually set guards to follow them when they knew they were probably being pursued.

Daniel, determined to abandon the trail and pursue a straighter, safer course, proceeded to lead the group of rescuers on his own path as silently and as rapidly as he could; however, the men still regularly crossed the Indians' trail. Assuming that rescuers were on their way, the girls had courageously and nonchalantly marked the trail over which they were being taken. They broke twigs, dropped small pieces of their clothing, dug their heels into muddy soil, broke limbs, and made signs that the rescuers would hopefully notice in their pursuit. When night arrived, the determined pursuers stopped to sleep before heading out again in the morning. At that point, they had followed the Indians approximately 35 miles.

By ten o'clock the next morning, a Tuesday, the rescuers reached Hinkston's Ford of the Licking River, where Daniel predicted that the Indians' trail would be found crossing that stream at a point just below it. Incredibly, that prediction proved to be true. Daniel's party traveled approximately 200 yards when they encountered fresh tracks and other signs that the Indians had become more relaxed in their efforts to cover their tracks. It was as though Daniel had a satellite in the heavens with a monitor that tracked the Indians' movements in the wilderness. If there was ever any doubt about Daniel's woodsmanship, this example of wilderness prowess should have proven his skill.

After crossing the river, the rescuers increased their speed to a slow trot. Eventually, they came upon a dead buffalo that had been deprived of its hump, out of which blood was continuing to drip. Daniel again made a remarkable prediction, guessing that the Indians would stop to cook the delicious buffalo meat as soon as they could find water. Soon after, the group also found a dead snake.

Approximately ten miles from Hinkston's Crossing, the trail suddenly disappeared. The Indians were able to obscure their tracks by wading a distance in the water. By these signs, however, Daniel knew that the Indians were nearby and probably preparing to eat the buffalo meat. With that, he cautioned his party to very stealthily approach the Indians while trying to avoid making any sounds that might alert them. His objective was to retrieve the girls safely and without giving the Indians an opportunity to kill them. He ordered that no man should fire his rifle without a signal from him.

A short time later, the rescuers came across the Indians, who were making a fire and preparing to cook the buffalo. They awaited a signal from Daniel to begin their rescue attempts. Unfortunately, that signal came in the form of an inadvertent discharge from the rifle of one of the pursuers, William D. Smith, who had discovered the Indian camp approximately 30 yards away.

The campsite immediately erupted into bedlam with confusion and disarray. At one point, Betsy was almost clubbed by one of Daniel's party, but was stopped by Daniel and reminded that she was one of theirs. In another instance, one of the Indians threw his tomahawk in the direction of one of the Calloway girls, which almost found its mark. The Indians eventually fled into the canebrakes, but two of them were mortally wounded. Once the situation was secure, the rescuers sat down to catch their breath. Relieved that the mission had been successful, they all spent time crying and expressing love and gratitude for each other and what they had been able to do.

Upon reaching Boonesborough, Daniel's group found Richard Calloway, who had just returned from the lower Blue Lick. He and his group of horsemen had reached Blue Lick, where they found clear evidence that the girls had been rescued, so they had returned to the fort. There must have been a happy celebration at Fort Boonesborough that day for the rescue and safe return of the three teenage girls. Richard, who, at first resented Daniel for taking charge and directing the rescue, was probably beyond grateful for Daniel's splendid display of woodsmanship, which probably saved the lives of his two lovely daughters.

We have read much about Daniel's sharp skills as a woodsman and how those skills developed over years of being in the wilderness. But never had so many people witnessed, firsthand, such a display of those skills as they saw that day. Perceiving the dangers, Daniel knew exactly where to go to find the three girls and how to rescue them when he got there. He had no way of knowing that his dramatic story of rescue would still be told more than 200 years later in places throughout the world.

The raid upon the Indians was so well planned, so sudden, and so effective that it completely caught the savages off guard. Those who were not killed fled to the canebrakes without even firing a shot, leaving behind their shotguns, ammunition, tomahawks, moccasins, and all other property. Upon entering their village, those Indians would have to tell the shameful story of how they had kidnapped three teenage girls but lost them over a meal of buffalo hump.

11
The Man Who Bought Hair

"The only thing worse than cruelty is delegated cruelty." —Matthew Scully

We will soon meet the man primarily responsible for spreading fear and grief among settlers on the frontiers across Virginia and Pennsylvania during part of the Revolutionary War. This same man, Henry Hamilton, also incited already angry Indians to kill and torture innocent men, women, and children.

Like most epics, the story of the settlement of Kentucky is a story of conquest. It details many struggles to conquer the vast wilderness and populate it with people who were looking for a better life —and ready to risk whatever was necessary to get it. Daniel did not regard the wilderness and the many challenges it offered as obstacles; rather, he seemed to always be at work, sharing the opportunities that he found all around him. What he did, he usually did alone, but one day he was to start receiving help from a young man he barely knew. In fact, this young man, George Rogers Clark, would eventually devote himself to the poor border settlers in their efforts to better themselves and their families. Over time, George managed to distinguish himself as one of the truly great men of Kentucky history through exploits that sometimes appeared as miracles.

By 1775, the War of Separation was already underway between the American colonies and Great Britain. The American Indian tribes to the north tended toward neutrality at first; however, they were increasingly alarmed by the steady loss to the Americans of their homeland and their hunting grounds. In that year, Great Britain appointed a former military officer to the post of lieutenant governor and superintendent of Indian affairs. Henry Hamilton, dubbed by George Rogers Clark as 'the hair-buyer' for his purchase of American scalps, was approached by some of the local Indians who were friendly toward the English. They asked for permission to make incursions against people who had settled on the frontiers of Kentucky and Pennsylvania. Having no authority from his superiors, Henry declined the request.

At the beginning of 1777, it was still the policy of Great Britain to keep the Indians above the Ohio River loyal to the interests of Great Britain and to be ready to join with the British against the Americans if and when they were needed. The Shawnee tribes, nevertheless, continued to attack settlements in Kentucky, and the Mingo Indians launched attacks against settlements in what is now West Virginia and southwestern Pennsylvania. Henry had suggested to London that it recruit parties of Indians under the supervision of 'proper leaders' to begin attacks against the Americans in order to divert attention from the ongoing Revolutionary War by creating multiple fronts.

Lord George Germain authorized Henry to enroll as many Indians of his district as he reasonably could; place proper persons at the head to avoid violence against peaceful inhabitants; and use the attack as a diversion to incite an alarm on the frontiers of Virginia and Pennsylvania. Within 60 days of receipt of Lord Germain's authorization, Henry assembled approximately 300 Indian warriors, divided them into 15 separate parties, and sent them off to make war on the exposed settlers.

Lord Germain's order to Henry to place 'proper persons' at the head of the savages, if it had been obeyed, might have prevented the violence that ensued; but it was not obeyed. In fact, Henry ended up appointing many persons of little or no character, who would only fight with the Indians in their cruelty.

At first, Daniel did not know that such strategy was under consideration, so he had no way of knowing the chilling effect it would have on new settlements of Kentucky if it was favorably considered. As it turned out, the British would implement such a policy from 1777 into 1782. The large numbers of angry Indians under the direction of barbarians such as Simon Girty, his two brothers, and others were loosed upon innocent men, women, and children—many of whom suffered great deprecations and sometimes horrible torture and brutality. It is amazing to consider that the settlers were not belligerents in the war and that many, if not most of them, were faithful to the Crown.

The policy, as it turned out, largely failed to achieve its purpose. It seems that requests to Virginia for troops and war supplies to defend against Indian attacks were being regularly denied so that the diversion of war power from the eastern front to the frontiers of Virginia and Pennsylvania did not often occur. Virginia wisely decided it needed to concentrate its resources in the east where the need was more compelling and the outcome more rewarding. Indian raids brought hundreds of casualties and virtually stopped settlement of Kentucky.

Henry took delight in the successes of the Indians in their raids on the border settlements as shown by correspondence he had with his superiors, Canadian Governor Guy Carleton and General Frederick Haldimand, in Detroit. In his report to them, Henry boasted that his policy of diversion was bearing fruit and that the Indians had brought to Detroit on January 15, 1778, "73 prisoners alive" and "129 scalps." He added that on September 27, 1778, they had delivered "34 prisoners and 81 scalps."

Some historians suggest that Henry had put a standing bounty on each white scalp—of any age or gender—that an Indian brought in. Other historians disagree, holding that there is no evidence to support it. Either way, Henry's own words are ample evidence that the Indian marauders could collect a bounty from somebody on the British side, and Henry, by his own words, acknowledged awareness of the practice. It appears that somebody in Canada was paying the Indians on a per scalp basis.

The conduct of affairs at Detroit was left largely to the discretion and judgment of Henry, and he was directed to use whatever power was necessary to insure British successes, including such steps as may be necessary to persuade the Indians to "take up the hatchet"against his Majesty's rebellious subjects in America. Initial dispatch of fifteen separate parties of Indians already mentioned resulted in the death or capture of men while working in the fields or out hunting. Women and children were burned in their houses. In other cases, entire families were carried away as prisoners. Other deprecations also occurred that are well-recognized and documented through testimonies of spies and prisoners, including the fact that scalps of victims were bought by the British at Detroit. Such atrocities were sufficiently established as to cause the Council of Virginia to include that charge among the charges preferred against Henry while he himself was a prisoner.

However, these acts of inhumanity cannot be attributed to all British officials. Lieutenant Governor Abbot appealed to General Carlton on June 8, 1778, to end the Indian outrages against innocent settlers, saying: "... It is not people in arms that Indians attack, but the poor inoffensive families who fly to the deserts to be out of trouble, and who are inhumanly butchered, sparing neither women nor children." One English military officer, Captain Bird, ordered by his superior to accompany the Indians on such a raid, discovered the Indians in the act of burning and torturing a white man. He scolded them:

> "You cowards! Is that all you can do to kill a poor innocent prisoner? You dare not show your faces where an army is, but there you are busy when you have nothing to fear. Get away from me. Never will I have to do with such as you are and be guilty in such a murder as you have committed."

The issue of using Indians to raid border settlers even reached Parliament. In reply to a statement by Lord Suffof, saying to the effect that Britain would be justified in doing anything necessary to be done to put down the insurrection, Lord Chatham deplored the enlistment of Indians:

> "But who is the man ... who has dared to authorize and associate to our arms the tomahawk and scalping-knife of the savage? ... What! To attribute the sanction of God and nature to the massacres of the Indian scalping-knife ... They shock every sentiment of honor. They shock me as a lover of honorable war and a detester of mur-

murderous barbarity. These abominable principles, and this more abominable avowal of them, demand a most decisive indignation."

Those abominations soon reached the conscience of George Rogers Clark, arousing in him the "most decisive indignation." As a relatively young man, 25 years of age, George would soon take upon himself the responsibility of improving the plight of settlers, a commitment that will lead him to a decisive victory over the so-called hair buyer and other victories on the political front, which ultimately advanced the needs of the settlers all along the frontiers. Although they did not work in tandem, George's deeds are inexorably tied to Daniel's efforts to settle the Kentucky wilderness and should be a part of any story of Daniel's life.

Besides the residents of Boonesborough, there were an estimated 200 hardy settlers at various locations in Kentucky who had made great sacrifices to settle the wilderness being claimed by Richard Henderson. One observer put the number of militia in Kentucky in 1775 at only 50, but that number increased to more than 1,000 by 1780. They had no government. They had no protector. They had no legal ownership in the property they had settled. They depended largely on game, wild roots and greens, berries, and the products of their gardens to live. A few of them, including Daniel, had resettled their wives and children into the awesome land that represented the last and foremost commitment to be made for the quest for a better life. These stalwarts lived in a communal anarchy, often cloistered together to protect themselves against the constant threat of Indian attacks, but too stubborn to give up their quest and move.

12
Military
Magic

"A zeal for the defense of their country led these heroes to the scene of action, though with a few men to attack a powerful army of experienced warriors." —Colonel Daniel Boone

We have already observed that while Richard Henderson was trying to advance his proprietary control over the territory that he "bought" from the Indians at the Sycamore Shoals Treaty, there appeared on the scene a young upstart Virginian who would soon make his mark on the troubled frontiers. This young Virginian belongs in any history that touches on the exploration, settlement, and development of early Kentucky.

George Rogers Clark was born in 1752 in Virginia, approximately 150 miles from the James River on a 400 acre farm. That is claimed by some to be the same year when the Boone family reached the

Yadkin Valley. George grew to be six feet, two inches tall—a giant for those days. He also had bright red hair and had a muscular build. Unlike Daniel, he apparently enjoyed farming and soon developed into an outdoorsman, a skilled marksman, woodsman, and hunter. His father described him as a man who was "quick as a cat . . . always landing on his feet."

George's achievements in school were modest, and he was more successful as a student in courses such as mathematics, history, and geography. His older brother, Jonathan, excelled in Latin and the classics, assuring him of more attention from the teacher. Among George's schoolmates were James Madison, the future president of the United States, and John Tyler, father of a future president. He frequently visited and had conversations with the brilliant George Mason, who grew to like him and who followed his career throughout his several years of public service.

George, by the time he was 19, had developed into a man who would command the attention and respect of other men he came into contact with. He would never have been mistaken as one of the tidewater planters with their prissy hand servants, and he had no difficulty communicating with men of substance and power — an ability that would serve him very soon in his dealings with such luminaries as Thomas Jefferson and Patrick Henry. Additionally, his courage would not fail to serve him on those occasions when he was about the business of leading common men into battle. Like so many others who had cropped on marginal lands and taught to make a profit, George knew the value of good land.

George, like most other men within earshot of a returning frontiersman, had heard tales of the lush Kentucky landscape—its fertile soil, plentiful game, and thick forests—and he soon began wanting to see those wonders for himself. He had learned the mathematics and instrumentation needed by competent surveyors, and he was prepared to use that knowledge to claim public lands for himself and others.

His years of farming on land supplied by his father had taught him to be attentive to such important features as elevations, water supply, and locations. He determined that he would soon visit the mysterious Kentucky, alone if necessary, make his way down the Ohio River, and explore the land there. Like so many other adventurers, George had that restlessness that drove him down unknown paths to unknown destinations.

As to when he first began his adventure upon the Ohio River, Reverend David Jones, Chaplain-

Elect of the new Continental Army, wrote in his journal:

> "I left Fort Pitt June 9, 1771, in the company of George Rogers Clark, a young gentlemen of Virginia who, with several others, were inclined to make tour of the new world."

George and some companions made their way to a place on the Kanawha River where George marked his first claim. After preparing the claim for spring, he returned to Virginia, browned and ready to tell his own story of adventure and exploration to family and friends. He did not stay at home very long, leaving for Kanawha River early the following spring. Between his first journey with Reverend Jones from Fort Pitt in June 1771 to the end of Lord Dunmore's War in 1774, George, while surveyor for the Ohio Company, went up and down the Ohio River and its tributaries for nearly five years, scouting for good land for his company and for himself. Soon, George became a face familiar to adventurers all up and down the river. He was well liked, quick with a smile, and ready to trade news and information regarding the river and its tributaries.

Settlement on both sides of the river grew dur-

during that period to such a volume as to cause alarm and consternation among the Indian tribes, who viewed the whole situation as a dangerous usurpation of their hunting rights. The same Indians began to make assaults upon the settlers' homesteads, and the settlers decided that they must become more aggressive in dealing with them.

A party of settlers prepared to retaliate with their own strikes. Governor Dunmore decided that the attack planned by the settlers was insufficient to convince the Indians that they must cease their raids. With that, he put together a retaliatory expedition against the offending Indians. In the course of fighting what became known as Dunmore's War, George was commissioned as "captain of the militia of Pittsburgh and its dependencies" by Lord Dunmore, the first of many military positions and honors that he would receive in the course of his military career. The war was short, lasting only a few months, and ended with the Indians suing for peace and surrendering all their rights to the land lying south of the Ohio. They also agreed that they would not cross the Ohio River.

As a result of George's work for the Ohio Company and his service during the war, he had become a respected and well-liked leader in the Ohio Valley. He was successful on Fish Creek of the Kanawha and was now ready to turn his attention to Kentucky. He had met and gained the respect of leaders whom he found in the wilderness, including Daniel Boone, Simon Kenton, and other adventurers whose names now frequently appear in books covering the history of early Kentucky.

Around this time, Richard Henderson, with his deed from the Cherokees, began causing concern among the settlers throughout Kentucky as to the effect of that deed on their claims to Kentucky lands. The settlers let it be known that Richard's claims would be resisted, and he tried several ways to incorporate the settlers into his proprietary plans even to the point of holding a convention to establish government and writing laws to govern it.

By then, George was a seasoned woodsman who was well-acquainted with a wilderness life. He was also aware of the problems faced by those who would try to make the Kentucky land their home. He arrived in Kentucky in 1775 and surveyed a new settlement, which he called Leestown, on the Kentucky River near Frankfort. Apparently, he was incensed by Richard's effort to expropriate the properties of settlers who had sacrificed to establish homesteads, and he became determined to do something to help the settlers preserve their claims.

George wrote the following about Richard's efforts to establish his claim:

"It was at this period that I first thought about concerning myself with the future of this country. I saw clearly that the proprietors (The Transylvania Company) were working their own ruin ... that their conduct would shortly exasperate the people and afford the opportunity to overthrow them."

George had been right. The people were exasperated and would use Transylvania Company's own plans as a reason to overthrow them. With that, George set about finding ways that the transaction with the Cherokee Indians might be nullified. He soon concluded that the best permanent solution — and one that would solve more of the settlers' problems —was to persuade Virginia to acknowledge its ownership of the western territory that encompassed Kentucky and make it a county, independent of Fincastle. Such legislation would make the settlements eligible for military protection by a paid and professional militia; it would also nullify Richard's deed. Creation of a county would carry with it the creation of a government structured in accord with Virginia's Constitution together with facilities and officers to carry those laws into effect.

George knew some of the most influential mem-

members of the Virginia Assembly, having been a former neighbor to Thomas Jefferson, a friend to George Mason, and acquainted with William Wythe, a friend of his father. He was well-positioned to present the issues and arguments to the leadership in the Virginia Assembly. While departing Williamsburg for Kentucky, he sent word to Harrodsburg that a convention would be held on June 6, 1776. However, he refrained from explaining the purpose of the meeting so that they could all hear what he had to say at the same time.

On June 6, George arrived at the convention, as planned, but he didn't show up until late in the afternoon. Unfortunately, the well attended convention had already adjourned. But while the members of the convention had met, they had selected George and John Gabriel Jones as delegates to the Virginia Assembly. The settlers also acted on a petition that the Virginia Assembly make Kentucky a county of Virginia. Once that business was taken care of, the delegates wasted no time in returning to Virginia, armed with the Kentucky proposals.

The men decided to travel south over the wet and treacherous trail along the Warrior's Path and through Cumberland Gap, which was a decision they quickly regretted. They saw signs of Indians and they were soon stricken with foot scald, a very painful condition caused by wearing wet moccasins over the rain drenched paths. Learning that the Virginia Assembly had adjourned, but that the governor of Virginia, Patrick Henry, was home in Williamsburg, George proceeded to the governor's home while John stopped on the Holston to rejoin George later. George found Governor Henry ill, but willing to see him.

He showed the governor the documents generated by the Harrodsburg Convention, which requested powder for use by the settlers in defending themselves, and also the petition for Kentucky to be incorporated into Virginia as a county. Governor Henry advised George that only the Virginia Assembly had the power to make Kentucky a new county, and he should resort to that body. With that said, the governor was very helpful and interested in George's ideas, and he offered him helpful advice and even assistance in formulating further plans.

George decided to stay in Williamsburg for the opening of the Virginia Assembly six weeks later when he would battle Richard Henderson over the Cherokee sale issue. The appeal to make Kentucky a new county of Virginia was met with strong and prolonged opposition from influential members of the convention, including Colonel Arthur Campbell, an influential delegate. Among the opposition were several of Richard's allies who knew that passage of the proposal meant sudden death for Richard's ambitious plans. However, on December 7, 1776, the Virginia Assembly passed a bill making a Kentucky a new county of Virginia. Additionally, George was made a major of the Virginia Militia, and he was put in charge of the defense of the new county. He was only 24 years old and must have been quite a sensation.

George had learned that powder, which Virginia had agreed to provide the frontier with, was at Pittsburgh. He and John then made plans to retrieve it on the way to Kentucky. They hastened to Pittsburgh, loaded the powder in boats, and were plowing down the Ohio when Indians appeared on the northern banks; they seemed interested in their movements.

George decided that it would be prudent to stash the powder in several different places where it would remain until a party originating in Harrodsburg could retrieve it. According to most historians, the powder was secretly buried around Limestone Harbor and was subsequently retrieved, but only after the Indians had murdered John in a skirmish. One scholar insists that the powder was hidden on one of the islands in the Ohio River near what is presently Manchester, Ohio.

After succeeding in making Kentucky a county,

George confronted another problem. By then, he had received intelligence that the British at Detroit, assisted by their forts at Vincennes, Kaskaskia, and Cahokia, were planning and carrying out Indian raids into Kentucky. He began to consider how those raids might be repelled and how to blunt any other similar attacks made upon the settlers in Kentucky. He believed in taking the battle to the enemy, which was a strategy that provided him with the ability to surprise the enemy—an advantage that the Indians felt to be very important in a battle. George would soon use that strategy to conquer the British forts.

13
A Triumph
of Cunning

"On the first day of January, 1778, I went with a party of 30 men to the Blue Licks, on Licking River, to make salt for the different garrisons in the country ... On the seventh day of February, as I was hunting, to procure meat for the company, I met with a party of 102 Indians, and two Frenchmen, on their march against Boonesborough, that place being particularly the object of the enemy." — Colonel Daniel Boone

Things at Boonesborough were back to normal after the rescue of Jemima and the two Calloway girls about a year-and-a-half earlier. But Daniel Boone, the hero, would soon be thought of as Daniel Boone, the traitor, in the minds of Richard Calloway and others who would accuse him of planning to deliver Boonesborough and its occupants to the savage Indians. That story full of drama, and no account of Daniel's life is complete without it.

Daniel had volunteered to accompany a crew of 27 men from Fort Boonesborough to go to the salt springs at Blue Lick. They planned to produce salt by boiling water from salty brine, a physically difficult and dangerous assignment. Blue Lick, like the other salt springs in the area, was frequented by large herds of bison and other animals; these animals required salt in their diets to survive. They would gather there, as needed, and lick the salty brine from the ground or take it from the spring water. Reducing it to salt was arduous because it required a crew to cut and gather firewood and keep fires going 24 hours a day. The heavy brine water was then boiled and evaporated in metal pots, leaving only a salty brine.

Salt springs tended to be located in remote places, and hostile Indians often visited them. The Indians resented the presence of white men on their hunting grounds. However, there were no salt pits in Kentucky; there were no stores at which to buy it; and there was no other place it could be acquired other than the settlements, which were located hundreds of miles away. Salt was needed in the process of curing meat to keep it from spoiling or being invaded by insects.

A settler must have among his provisions a plentiful supply of cured meat free of spoilage and insect invasion. Having no refrigeration or other means of preserving it, it had to be 'cured' to keep it from spoiling by bathing it in a bath of pure salt. If the supply of salt was exhausted, there could be no meat for consumption during the time when the cured meat was not available and they would have to live on fresh meat if it was available.

The springs at Blue Lick were one of the better sources for saltwater in middle Kentucky, but that saltwater source was located quite a distance from Fort Boonesborough. There were other closer salt springs; however, they did not yield enough salt water to make their use worthwhile. The springs at Blue Lick were favored because they produced approximately 10,000 gallons of salt water a day—a marginal but acceptable volume. The production of a single bushel of salt required that several hundred gallons of spring water be boiled, and the water evaporated. If the springs from which the salt solution was taken had low salt content, workers would need to boil down a greater quantity of water.

The salt crew chose early January to travel to the salt springs with the hopes of not encountering Indians during the wintertime. The plan was to make enough salt to last Fort Boonesborough a full year, which was an ambitious undertaking. The finished salt would be sent by horseback to Boonesborough; the salt makers would be given a vacation from the hard work; and other workers would replace them until they, too, could be rotated back to the fort. Daniel had the responsibility for keeping the twenty-seven-man crew supplied with fresh meat. That was difficult, though, due to his knowledge of the countryside around Blue Lick and other places where most of the game congregated for forage.

It was not a good day. While Daniel had been hunting, he encountered snow that had frozen into ice after it hit the ground, making it difficult to walk. He killed and field-dressed a young buffalo, and then strapped its carcass to his horse to be led by foot to the camp at Blue Lick. On his way back to the salt camp, he discovered a party of four Indians following him with the obvious intent of killing him or taking him prisoner. He tried to drop the heavy load of buffalo from the horse so he could flee, but was unable to do it because his knife was frozen into its sheath. He was unable to cut the straps that held the carcass to his horse. He tried to escape on foot into the woods to elude the younger and more agile Indians, but was unable to outrun them.

Realizing that the Indians would overtake and kill him, Daniel knew that his best hope of surviving was to surrender. He did so by leaning his rifle against a tree where the Indians could see it. The four Indians had originally been on their way to tell their chief, Chief Blackfish, that they had observed a group of white men making salt at the lower Blue Licks. With Daniel's capture, they now had something else to tell him.

When they arrived at the Shawnee camp, the warriors erupted into cheers and celebration. Daniel was surprised and intimidated by the size of the Indian party. Shawnees usually avoided conflict until the warmer months; they often remained in their villages through the winter. While at the Shawnee camp, Daniel learned that the Shawnees were on their way to attack Boonesborough with a force of 120 warriors—large enough to take the fort with awful consequences to its inhabitants, including his wife, Rebecca, and his family.

The attack was planned to avenge the wanton murder of their revered Chief Cornstalk. The chief had been on a mission of peace at the time of his recent murder by whites. On October 10, 1774, he had led eleven hundred Indian braves against colonial troops. After his defeat, however, he pursued a peace policy, forbidding his braves to interfere with the whites or molest them. During the American Revolution in 1777, Chief Cornstalk returned to

Point Pleasant to warn settlers of British plans to attack them, but he was seized and imprisoned as a hostage. A group of soldiers entered the room where he was imprisoned, and he calmly faced his slayers. He was killed, along with his son and two companions.

Daniel, seeing the size of the Indian army, knowing their anger and quest for revenge, and knowing that the unfinished fort was the object of the Indians' hostilities, realized the gravity of the threat of siege to the lives of the settlers at Fort Boonesborough. But that's not all. He also knew that if something wasn't done to prevent it, the angry Indians would fall upon his 27 salt makers, taking them by surprise and undoubtedly slaughtering them all. But what could he do? He was only one man against 120 angry warriors, and it was up to him to do something to avoid the carnage. He knew he had to quickly think of a way to save himself, the salt makers, and the women and children at Boonesborough.

Daniel soon had an opportunity to confer with Chief Blackfish. In that meeting, Daniel wasted no time ingratiating himself to Chief Blackfish and offering him a plan that he could not easily refuse. He could return to his villages victorious and not risk losing a single warrior. Daniel convinced Chief

Blackfish that there were mostly women and children at the fort, and that if they were made prisoners and marched to the Shawnee town in inclement weather, many would die. Ultimately, the Indians would lose the British bounty given for live prisoners.

As Chief Blackfish contemplated Daniel's words, Daniel continued. He promised that if the Indians agreed to treat them fairly and not make them run the gauntlet — the Shawnees' favorite sport — he would agree to surrender the salt crew without resistance. He also promised that if the Shawnees would abandon the plan to assault Boonesborough and wait for the springtime, which would be more favorable weather for traveling, to remove the women and children, he would surrender the fort to the Indians without resistance. In the end, they could all live together in peace and harmony. The terms of surrender were agreed to and accepted by the gullible Chief Blackfish, and the salt makers were saved from the tomahawk and the scalping knife.

On Sunday, February 8, 1778, the salt boilers rested. The salt springs had flooded, and the rising water made it impossible to collect brine to be boiled. At that point, the salt-making crew consisted of 27 men. They were lying around on their blankets, warming themselves, when they suddenly saw the Indians approaching them. Immediately, the men jumped to their feet, seized their guns, and made ready for battle. Daniel then appeared and ordered the crew to hold their fire. He told the men that he was captive of a large party of armed Indians on their way to attack Boonesborough.

He also told them that the Indians were prepared to engage the fort, and that if they did, they would all be killed. He said that the chief had promised that if they surrendered, they would be treated fairly, taken to the villages as prisoners, and they would not be forced to run the gauntlet. The men were already well acquainted with Daniel; they trusted him and promptly obeyed him.

After the surrender of the salt makers, the Indians held a council wherein it was proposed that they should kill all the prisoners, except Daniel, and that he should be made to lead them to Fort Boonesborough and compel them to surrender as he had done with the salt makers. Several Indians spoke at the council, and it appeared that the vote would be close. A black Indian, Pompay, sat close to Daniel and whispered translations of what was being said. Finally, after approximately two hours of speeches, Chief Blackfish let Daniel make a closing speech:

"Brothers! What I have promised you, I can much better fulfill in the spring than now. Then the weather will be warm, and the women and children can travel from Boonesborough to the Indian towns, and all live with you as one people. You have got all my young men; to kill them, as has been suggested, would displease the Great Spirit, and you could not then expect future success in hunting nor war. If you spare them, they will make you fine warriors, and excellent hunters to kill game for your squaws and children. These young men have done you no harm, they were engaged in a peaceful occupation, and unresistingly surrendered upon my assurance that such a course was the only safe one for them; and I consented to their capitulation on the express condition that they should be made prisoners of war and treated well. I now appeal both to your honor and your humanity; spare them, and the Great Spirit will smile upon you."

Daniel was holding the lives of 27 men in his hands. Those men were dependent on the eloquence of a man with no education and who could hardly read his own name—a man armed only with cunning and resolve. After Daniel's speech, the council voted 61 to 59 in favor of mercy. Until Daniel rose and made his speech, the salt makers did not realize the seriousness of the situation and that their lives, and the lives of their families, would depend solely on Daniel's ability to persuade the Indians to abandon their raid on Fort Boonesborough. Immediately, after the decision of the council, the Indians began preparations to return to Little Chillicothe. First, they spilled all of the salt that had been produced and scattered it around the area. Then they divided cooking kettles, rifles, ammunition, axes, and other implements to be carried to the village. After traveling a distance, the parties eventually stopped for the evening. As it began to get dark, Daniel noticed that a party of Indians was clearing the snow out of a long track and preparing what looked like a gauntlet track.

He located Pompay and reminded him of Chief Blackfish's promise, and they went to Chief Blackfish together for an explanation. Chief Blackfish, appearing amused, reminded Daniel that the promise of fair treatment and exemption from running the gauntlet applied only to the salt makers—not to him. Daniel decided to go along with the dangerous sport rather than reopen the agreement he worked out with Chief Blackfish and the council.

Daniel was soon subjected to that cruel ritual of the gauntlet. The Shawnees lined up on either side of the cleared path, armed with lethal weapons, tomahawks, clubs, and almost everything else. When the signal was made, Daniel entered into the fray by dodging, sidestepping, and avoiding the blows with such agility that it appeared he was going to get through the gauntlet untouched. However, he was hit several times and received injuries to his head that produced enough blood to impair his vision. Near the end of the run, a brave stepped out, blocking his way. Daniel made a charge and butted him in his belly, causing him to stumble into the snow. The Indian dusted the snow from his buffalo cape and someone called him a "dumb squaw." The Indian grinned good naturedly at the jab. Later, other salt makers were also subjected to the gauntlet, but all of them escaped without serious injury.

The next day, the Indians left with their captives for Little Chillicothe. During that long journey, the temperature remained so cold that some of the Indians sustained frostbite. They had no food and were confined to eating white oak bark because of the absence of game, owing to the inclement weather. After ten days, during which all of the travelers suffered, the group reached their final destination..

The Indians at Little Chillicothe warmly greeted the travelers with a celebration, which included a traditional war dance, and they wasted no time in adopting 16 of the salt makers. Daniel was adopted as a son of Chief Blackfish, and he was given the In-

Indian name, Sheltowee, which stands for "Big Turtle." He was also promptly introduced to his new mother, his two little sisters, and his new Indian home.

The Indian adoption ceremony was not a silly ritual. To the contrary, once the adoption was complete, the adoptee became a member of the adopting family and of the tribe. The adoptee would then be regarded in the same way as his or her new brothers, sisters, and parents without any showing of preference. About a month after the group had arrived at Little Chillicothe, Daniel learned that the ten captives who had not been adopted were going to be taken by Chief Blackfish to Detroit—and that he must go along, too.

14
Boone with Blackfish in Detroit

"During our travels, the Indians entertained me well; and their affection for me was so great, that they utterly refused to leave me there with the others, although the Governor offered them one hundred pounds sterling for me, on purpose to give me a parole to go home." —Colonel Daniel Boone

Soon after Daniel arrived in Detroit with Chief Blackfish, Lieutenant Governor Henry Hamilton sent for him to come to his quarters. After friendly greetings and an exchange of pleasantries, Henry expressed regret that Daniel had been taken into custody, and it was his intent to appeal to the Shawnees for his release. By the time of that meeting, however, Daniel had already been adopted into Chief Blackfish's family as his son, and the chief was apparently happy with that. It has been said that Daniel promised Henry to be friendly to the British cause, and that he again agreed to give up the people at Boonesborough.

Henry may also have offered Chief Blackfish one hundred pounds for Daniel's release, but the chief rejected it. Unable to redeem him, Henry still gave him a horse, bridle, and blankets with a small supply of silver to trade with the Indians. That offer was gratefully accepted even though it was little pay for the suffering that he had endured at the hands of the British. Imagine, though, the consternation of his fellow captives when word got around Detroit that the man who had surrendered them to that awful imprisonment was running around Detroit on a horse that came from the king's commissary.

Daniel's conduct during his imprisonment aroused suspicion by some of his fellow prisoners that he had 'gone over' to the British and had delivered them into captivity to promote British causes. It was understandable that they might have such suspicions for several reasons. He could be seen riding a horse, unattended, while wearing Indian clothing given to him out of the king's storehouse. He had been summoned to the governor's quarters *alone* for reasons unknown to them. Chief Blackfish's family had adopted Daniel as a son, and he had happily cooperated by having his hair plucked out by squaws and his white man's blood scrubbed out, making him an Indian. He was given liberty to hunt without supervision and had been entrusted with a gun and ammunition. He had also been given trinkets of silver, which he was permitted to exchange for goods among the Indians. It may readily appear to anybody that something was wrong and that their leader had defected to the enemy.

Daniel, in his defense, later insisted that his conduct was simply a ruse to make it possible for him to escape to Boonesborough and prepare the fort against siege by the Indians. There is no doubt that by delivering the salt makers into the hands of Chief Blackfish, and his promise to deliver Boonesborough to the Indians in the spring, saved the lives of many, if not all, of the men, women, and children at Boonesborough.

After spending approximately a month in Detroit, Daniel headed back to Little Chillicothe with Chief Blackfish, arriving comfortably on the horse Henry provided for him. Upon his return to Little Chillicothe, Daniel seemed to fit very well into his role as a captive.

As mentioned, Daniel was entrusted with a gun and a small amount of ammunition from time to time, and he was allowed to go hunting by himself. He was only given a small amount of ammunition at first, but the allotment of powder and lead was increased as time went on and as Chief Blackfish became more convinced of Daniel's trustworthiness. He was careful to use the ammunition wisely and share the results of any hunt with his new family. He would also conserve powder by charging his rifle with a reduced load of powder and build a stockpile for future use.

Sometime in June, Chief Blackfish went to a location on the Scioto River to make salt from boiling spring water, and he took Daniel along with him. Daniel was not with the salt making party that day. Instead, he was with his Indian mother and some other squaws. Chief Blackfish had chased turkeys about a mile and a half into a tree and was distracted by efforts to shoot them down.

Daniel had seen a large gathering of Indian warriors at the salt springs, which had just returned from an expedition against two American forts. Daniel thought that that assemblage included warriors who were planning to head toward Fort Boonesborough in the expected siege, meaning there was not much time remaining for him to act. He knew that such a raid upon the fort was planned and preparations were already being made. This knowledge made his escape more imperative. This was his opportunity. He had moccasins, blankets, and a horse with a bridle and saddle that was refreshed for travel.

He observed his Indian mother and the group of squaws for a moment; they were busy tending to the horses packed with salt and boiling kettles, ready to return to the village. Suddenly, Daniel cut the rope that held the brass kettles to his horse, which immediately startled his Indian mother. She asked him what he was going to do. He replied that he was going to see his squaw and children and that he would soon return with them to live among his brothers and sisters. She warned him that he must not go because Chief Blackfish would be angry. He would surely find him and bring him back. She also told him that he would get lost and would not have food or shelter for himself. At the same time, the other squaws sounded an alarm, giving notice to Chief Blackfish and the Indians that something was happening. With that, Daniel spurred his horse and took off, very quickly disappearing out of sight of potential pursuers.

Chief Blackfish followed his trail for some distance, but then shortly returned, predicting that Daniel would get lost. Daniel continued riding his horse at a quick pace until around noon time the following day. The pace had been so grueling for so long that the horse eventually went lame and could not proceed further. Daniel removed the saddle, turned the horse loose, and started toward Boonesborough on foot, concealing his trail as he went along. He proceeded on foot until he reached the Ohio River, where he then improvised a raft by tying pieces of wood together with a rope made out of grapevines. He swam across, pushing it along ahead of him.

Emerging from the water, Daniel continued on foot until he decided to rest. After creating a makeshift camp and getting some much needed sleep, he awoke the next morning to find that his feet were scalded from his travels. Knowing that he had to keep moving, he treated them by making a poultice from oak bark. Once he was done doing that, he realized that he was very hungry, not having eaten for some considerable time.

He was able to take the gun he had fashioned from parts that he had squirreled away while being imprisoned and use it to kill a bison, reserving the tongue for his young ten year old son, Daniel. With his strength somewhat restored, he continued his trek toward Boonesborough. Four days and 140 miles later, he finally arrived at Boonesborough. Imagine his disappointment upon finding that Rebecca was not there to greet him. Thinking he was dead, Rebecca and all the children had returned to the settlement, except for Jemima, who had remained at the fort.

This story is another case of high drama in the life of Daniel Boone. He had walked 140 miles in four days; rode so hard that he exhausted his horse; swam across the Ohio River, pushing along an improvised raft; made a functional gun out of a few pieces of scrap; had one little piece of buffalo meat during that time; and finally returned home after four and a half months of captivity, only to find his family had given him up for dead. Added to that was his self imposed responsibility for saving the lives of scores of men, women, and children at Fort Boonesborough.

Upon his return, Daniel was surprised that the men of Boonesborough had done almost nothing to improve Fort Boonesborough's defenses against siege, especially after all the warnings of impending Indian raids from the north. Without wasting any time, he quickly set about examining the fort's fortifications and embarked on a plan to repair it to withstand an assault. In other words, Daniel did what he did best. He took charge and repaired the fort's defenses in approximately ten days. It must have been an inspiring scene to watch with axes singing, workhorses snorting, and men groaning and working hard to strengthen the fort, all under the leadership of the man from the Yadkin Valley.

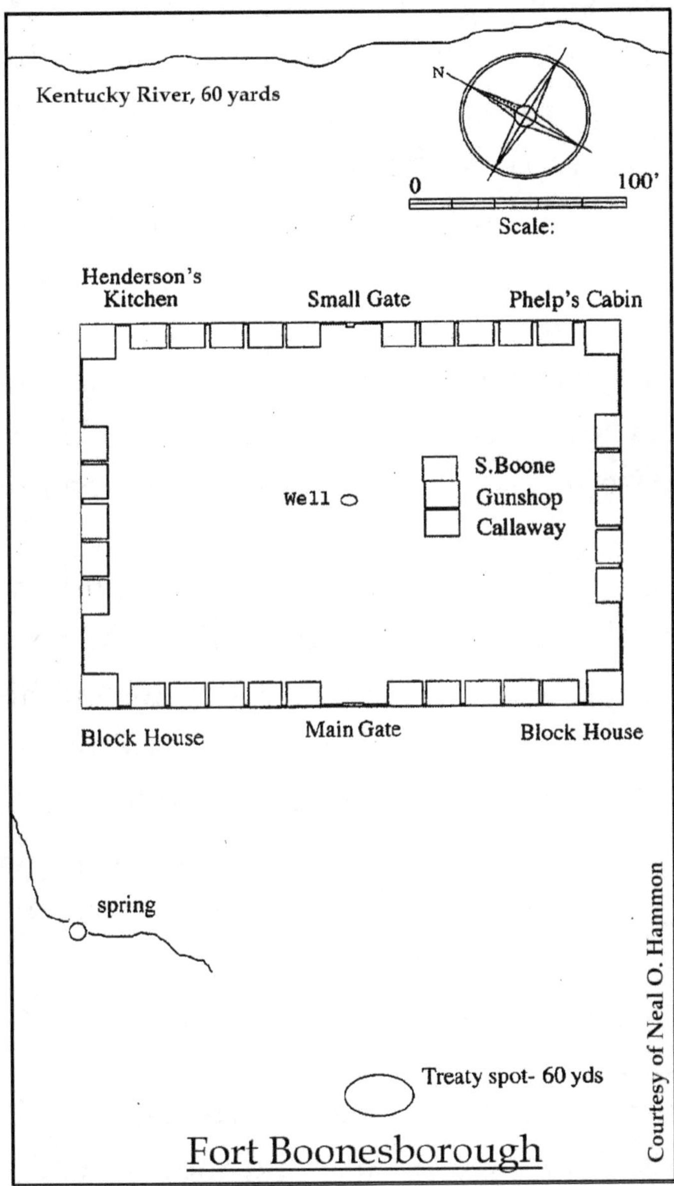

In addition to repairing and completing the palisades, which was a matter of greatest importance in making the fort secure against a long siege, work was done on the other fortifications. The men of Fort Boonesborough even started a new well to supplement their supply of water, which was absolutely necessary for survival in a long siege. At times during the repairs, the settlement received reports that the Indians were on their way; however, these reports proved to be wrong. Shortly before the repairs were completed, they received word from another escaped prisoner from Little Chillicothe that Chief Blackfish had postponed the siege. He wanted to increase the size of his force before heading that way.

In spite of all that Daniel had seen and endured up until that point, it was expected that he would be looking around for further action to cool his restlessness. Not content with merely waiting for the Indians to arrive and lay siege to the fort, he decided to do some raiding of his own. He proposed that a party be formed to make an incursion into the Indians' territory north of the Ohio River where there might be horses, furs and skins, and a large cache of other property.

Approximately 30 men were tempted by the prospect of a quick reward, and they agreed to join the expedition without any hesitation. However, Richard Calloway hesitated, contending that it would be a foolish venture and one that might ex-

expose Boonesborough to greater threats from the Indian marauders. He also added that it would be a waste of ammunition and other assets needed for defense of the fort.

Among the thirty men who were still willing to go on the expedition were Simon Kenton, Alexander Montgomery, and various other skilled and experienced woodsmen of Daniel's caliber. As the expedition got under way, however, approximately ten men decided to leave and return to Fort Boonesborough. Even with 20 men, they were enough of a force to contend with the usual band of Indians they might encounter.

With that, Daniel and his group crossed the Ohio River without incident and entered the Scioto Valley. Shortly after entering the valley, the party encountered a group of approximately 30 warriors, who had obviously intended to join in the siege of Boonesborough. After a fierce fight, Daniel's men killed one Indian and wounded several others, and they left with three Indian horses and a quantity of Indian plunder.

The party soon reached a point about four miles distant from Paint Creek, their target. Simon and Alexander scouted the town and found there were no warriors. It was apparent from this and other intelligence that the Indians were putting together a large force. It also seemed as if they were preparing to invade Boonesborough immediately. They quickly left for Kentucky, intent on arriving at Boonesborough before the Indians did. They managed to reach Boonesborough without further encounters.

As it turned out, contrary to Richard's concerns, the brief expedition revealed important intelligence that confirmed the Indians were indeed on their way. Daniel and his men were also able to learn the approximate size of the Indians' force, the direction of their movements, and the approximate time of their arrival. All of that information was extremely useful to the Boonesborough defenders, and it cost them nothing. The town took the remaining time to repair weapons, mold bullets, and make sure an adequate supply of water was available.

When the Indians finally arrived, they came with a large supply of ammunition, and even war paint. Henry Hamilton, in one report, recorded the purchase of approximately eighteen hundred scalping knives for use in such expeditions—a callous disregard for the lives and safety of unoffending men, women, and children.

The next morning, the Indians arrived under the colors of Great Britain and France, displaying a flag of truce. One of the Indian party members, the black slave named Pompay, appeared. He waved a flag and called out to the fort, asking if Captain Boone was there. The settlers did not immediately answer. When he called out a second time, Daniel answered, confirming that he was there. Pompay advised Daniel that he had letters from Lieutenant Governor Hamilton, and he should come out into the open and receive them. Of course, Daniel immediately refused to do that. He told Pompay that he should deliver the letters to the fort. Then Chief Blackfish stepped forward, addressing Daniel by his adoptive name, Sheltowee. He, too, asked for Daniel to come out. Daniel agreed, walked out of the fort, and was taken to see the chief.

It was their first meeting since Daniel's flight from Little Chillicothe, and Chief Blackfish appeared friendly. He cordially shook Daniel's hand and inquired about his health. The chief then asked why Daniel had run away. Daniel sadly told him that he was missing his family and had to see them. Chief Blackfish replied that if he had only told him that, he would have let him go and made it possible for him to see his family.

Chief Blackfish delivered Henry's letters in which he warned that resisting might result in massacre. Daniel advised the chief that he was no longer in command at the fort. As proof, he then went into the fort and brought with him Major William Bailey Smith, who was wearing a bright-colored uniform, complete with a military hat that was decorated with ostrich feathers. It must have been clear that Major Smith was, indeed, the commander of Boonesborough. Chief Blackfish believed him, and then told Daniel his warriors were hungry. He was told he could have whatever he needed, but was asked to not let any food go to waste.

After discussion among the settlers, the people of Fort Boonesborough agreed unanimously to defend the fort "to the last extremity," which meant even to the death of the last man, woman, and child. There would be no surrender. They all recognized, however, that the longer they could delay the consequences of their decision, the better it would be for all of them. They knew that they needed to bargain with the Indians as long as the Indians would permit it.

Six days of tedious negotiations between Fort Boonesborough and the Indians followed, provoking anger and outrage. During the negotiations, a number of proposals were made, primarily by the Indian delegation, for settling the dispute over the surrender of the fort. Each of those proposals was rejected. Finally, on the last day before the onset of battle, the Indians finally proposed a solution to which the settlers agreed. It was to be signed the following day.

The agreement provided in substance that the settlers, since they had bought the land from the

Cherokees, should be allowed to keep it; that the Ohio River should become the boundary between the whites and the Indians; and that the settlers would come under Henry's authority, taking an oath of obedience to the British. Chief Blackfish prescribed that eighteen warriors would be entitled to accompany him so as to give each of the various tribes present a representative at the signing. That left the settlers with only half as many representatives as the Indians would have to attend the signing.

Chief Blackfish advised the negotiators that it was customary among Indians to consummate such an agreement with a complex ceremony. To Daniel, such an event seemed to be a ruse to put the negotiators in a position of danger. He had taken the precaution to position armed riflemen with rifles loaded and cocked on the palisades with instructions to fire into the group of negotiators at the first sign of trouble, reasoning that they had a two to one chance of hitting an Indian.

As usual, Daniel was right. The Indians used the ceremony in an attempt to imprison the out-manned settlers, which they quickly recognized. They responded immediately, each breaking away from his attackers and making a run to the safety of the stockade. The riflemen in the stockade began to fire, and each Indian responded with his own fire from the underbrush. Every settler escaped without injury, except for Daniel's younger brother, Squire, Jr., who received a wound to his shoulder.

Following the foiled attempt by the Indians, they devised several stratagems designed to evict the occupants from the fort, including attempts to lure them outside the fort by appearing to have left when they had only retreated and were lying in ambush; attempting to burn the fort in various ways; and constructing a tunnel under the wall of the fort on the river side. Those attempts all failed, and the fort remained secure until the nine day siege was discontinued. Finally, the settlers were safe again within its walls. The account revealed that two defenders had been killed and four were wounded. Thirty seven Indian attackers had been killed.

After the Indian threat was over, it came time for Benjamin Logan and Richard Calloway to act on what they considered to be traitorous conduct on Daniel's part. They preferred formal charges against him before a militia tribunal and specified the charges:

"i. That Boone had taken out 26 men to
make salt at the Blue Licks, and the Indians
had caught him trapping for beaver ten

miles below on Licking, and voluntarily surrendered his men at the Licks to the enemy.

"ii. That when a prisoner, he engaged with Gov. Hamilton to surrender the people of Boonesborough, to be removed to Detroit, and lived under British protection and jurisdiction.

"iii. That returning from captivity, he encouraged a party of men to accompany him to the Paint Lick Town, weakening the garrison at a time when the arrival of an Indian army was daily expected to attack the fort.

"iv. That preceding the attack on Boonesborough, he was willing to take the officers of the fort, on pretence of making peace, to the Indian camp, beyond the protection of the guns of the garrison."

At the court martial hearing, Daniel defended himself by repeatedly assuring the assembly that his conduct while he was in Detroit as a prisoner had been a ploy to gain his freedom in order to return to the fort, strengthen its defenses, and save the settlers from extinction. He confirmed that he had surrendered the salt makers to the Indians in order to try and have their lives spared. The outcome was a favorable acquittal on all charges.

Daniel's conduct was vindicated by the action of the tribunal, promoting him to the rank of major. Apparently, someone stole the transcript of the court martial proceedings if there ever was one.

15
Ambush at Blue Licks

"I cannot reflect upon this dreadful scene, but sorrow fills my heart. A zeal for the defense of their country led these heroes to the scene of action, though with a few men to attack a powerful army of experienced warriors. When we gave way, they pursued us with the utmost eagerness, and in every quarter spread destruction." —Colonel Daniel Boone

After his acquittal of all charges under his court martial in the fall of 1778, a triumphant Daniel Boone wasted no time returning to the Yadkin Valley to be reunited with Rebecca and his children. In the four and a half months since the Shawnees had imprisoned him, he had faced problems that would have tested the strength and resolve of any man. He had saved the salt crew from certain death; he had somehow charmed his captors into believing that he might be a friend; he had escaped from captivity by cunning stratagem; he was instrumental in repulsing the Indian siege on Fort Boonesborough, probably saving the lives of many of its occupants; and he was exonerated from charges of treason made against him.

The stories of his exploits, which were sometimes heroic, were being noticed all around the border settlements. They were also being increasingly embellished with legend and myth. In a few short years on the Yadkin, he had grown from a 15 year-old boy, killing squirrels with a club, to a colonel in the militia, leading desperate men into battle against savage Indians. Suddenly, the truant father and husband had become a local curiosity whose reputation for daring adventures was spreading rapidly.

One thing about Daniel had not changed, though. He continued to dream of having a homestead in Kentucky with fertile soil, fresh rivers and streams, plenty of game, and solitude not to be found anywhere else; a place large enough that he could settle all his children around him and provide land to them for their future. That dream had already brought him twice from the Yadkin Valley into Kentucky, leading two different parties of settlers — a cavalcade of dreamers on their way to the so called Promised Land. It had also brought him profound grief.

At 45, here he was again, preparing to shepherd a third group of family and friends into Eden toward their own personal version of that dream. He used the summer of 1779 to recruit settlers within the Yadkin Valley for yet another venture into Kentucky. This time, he would take advantage of new Virginia land laws, which had been enacted to bring order to the chaotic provisions that had caused so much confusion and disarray in the past.

Those laws provided that a person who had improved a tract of land and raised a crop of corn before January 1, 1778, could claim 400 acres at a cost of two dollars and 25 cents per 100 acres. Others of the household could claim 1,000 at forty dollars per one 100 acres. The Virginia Land Commission had scheduled meetings during the winter of 1779 to 1780 to give claimants an opportunity to formally establish those claims, and several of the new immigrants intended to appear at those hearings to claim land under those laws. Altogether, the party consisted of approximately one hundred people, nearly all of them from the Yadkin Valley, and several members of the close Bryan family. Many of the immigrants were poor with their meager possessions strapped to their backs, children at their heels, trudging along barefooted. It is said that the grandfather of Abraham Lincoln was included among the migrants.

There were few men like Daniel Boone. He would confidently lead settlers along hundreds of miles of narrow Indian paths, across rivers, over bruising rock, and through briars and canebrakes. He would sleep nights around the same campfires, and he would be up before daylight, finding his way down the narrow pathways in search of Indians while at the same time scouting for that night's campsite. He could be seen in the late afternoon hours after returning from the day's hunt, perched on a fallen log, cleaning his rifle and filling his powder horn and shot bag, attentive to every sound from the forest. In the evening hours before bedtime, he liked to sit around the campfires and tell stories to wide eyed children and grownups alike.

Once the group of travelers arrived at their destination, Daniel would do what he could to help the new Kentuckians construct shelters for their families, clear fields, and plant crops. At the same time, he would always keep a lookout for Indians. For well over 200 years, people have applauded Daniel's willingness to share the untouched wilderness of Kentucky with others who expressed the slightest interest, all without pay. Incredible as it may seem in this day of fees, fares, and freeloaders, there is no record of Daniel having accepted a dime for passage. For him to charge for passage would have been as unthinkable as Moses charging the Hebrews for passage to the Promised Land.

In late fall 1779, the party of settlers arrived at Fort Boonesborough only to find the same Boonesborough that Daniel had left—one that had received little by way of repair since the siege. The squalor and the stench apparently convinced the Bryans to leave the fort and build their own station at a new location fairly close by, which they eventually called Bryan Station.

Soon after, Daniel, determined to leave Boonesborough where he no longer felt at ease, and after appearing before the Land Commission, led a group of Boones and others to a location approximately six miles from Boonesborough where he had buildings for shelter waiting. During their stay at the new Boone Station, the settlers witnessed one of the severest winters in history. Many of the animals froze to death. Even livestock and other game, accustomed to survival under harsh winter conditions, were unable to endure the freezing temperatures; many of them died. After the weather moderated, however, Boone Station began to take shape and provided permanent shelters for its new occupants, mostly Daniel's children, and others of the Boone clan.

Daniel attended hearings of the newly formed Virginia Land Commission, and he easily established claims to 1,400 acres for himself, 1,000 acres for George, his brother, and 1,400 acres for Israel, his son. It was at this point that Daniel, the hunter, turned his attention to the business of dealing in the acquisition of Kentucky land. His unique knowledge of Kentucky—gained from more than twelve years of hunting and exploring its rugged landscape —was not to be found in any other man.

Daniel was increasingly asked to perform services for newcomers and speculators, and the demand for his knowledge was continually increasing. With time, he realized that he might be able to make land acquisitions his full-time business. Unfortunately, around that same time, Daniel had some bad luck. While on his way to the Virginia capital at Williamsburg to buy preemption warrants for himself and others, he was robbed of the money, which had been entrusted to him. According to historians, he had stopped at an inn to spend the night, and an unknown thief pilfered his saddlebags, taking approximately 5,600 pounds in Virginia paper money, or about 20 pounds in silver.

That money was never recovered. Poor Daniel was left with accusations of dishonesty by a few of his clients. However, the incident showed the esteem in which he was held by some of his neighbors. The value of the money stolen is difficult to assess, but it may be considerably less than the amount reported to have been taken.

After serving out a term in the Virginia General Assembly, Daniel returned to Kentucky in the spring of 1782. The long war between the Indians and the settlers had lasted beyond Great Britain's surrender and into the Armistice Negotiations. There was still plenty of anger and hatred on both sides of the Indian problems to fuel the conflict, and there was always Major De Peyster, Henry Hamilton's successor as Lieutenant Governor of Detroit, to light the match.

Following the lead of Henry, the major would continue to send agents to the Indians, encouraging them to attack on Kentucky's border settlements. He provided a large quantity of weapons for use by 700 Indians during an assault on the Kentucky settlements at a cost of approximately 50,000 pounds sterling. The plan was to assault Ruddles Station, one of the Northern settlements. The assault successfully destroyed Ruddles Station by battering the fort with heavy cannons. Martin's Station was next in line for destruction.

Two other forts that received word that they would also be attacked burned their homes and quickly fled. Captain Bird, who found himself unable to control the savages, abandoned the expedition and returned to Detroit out of concern for the 300 prisoners that he had in custody. In retaliation for these and other Indian attacks, General George Rogers Clark gathered an army of approximately 1,000 men and attacked the Shawnees, burning Little Chillicothe and other Indian villages, and committing dreadful atrocities against the occupants of those villages.

Daniel was with George on the expedition against the Indians in 1781, and he was the ranking militia officer in Fayette County. Colonel John Todd had been serving as legislator at the capital in Richmond. Daniel described the effect of these raids in his autobiography, which was dictated to John Filson:

"This campaign (the expedition of General Clark against Old Chelicothe) in some measure damped the spirits of the Indians, and made them sensible of our superiority. Their connections were dissolved, their armies scattered and a future invasion put entirely out of their power, yet they continued to practice mischief secretly upon the inhabitants, in exposed parts of the country."

In August 1782, an army of warriors had gathered north of the Ohio River. The army planned to attack Kentucky settlements with the hopes of dealing a decisive blow against the many settlers and settlements that had grown up on the Kentucky frontier in recent years. The army consisted of a number of tribes north of the Ohio, including Delaware, the Mingo Indians, Miami, the Shawnees, and the Cherokees. Also attending the gathering was Simon Girty, the hated white Indian, and various officers of the British Army.

Before departing for Kentucky, Simon —who, as a child, had been raised as an Indian and whose loyalties were firmly with them —made an impassioned speech that many have praised as a well expressed statement of the many wrongs done to the suffering Indians since the coming of the white man. The concluding paragraph of that speech is eloquent:

"Brothers, the intruders on your lands exult in the success that has crowned their flagitious acts ... They are planting fruit trees and ploughing the lands where not long since were the cane break and the clover field. Was there a voice in the trees of the forest, or articulate sounds in the gurgling waters, every part of this country would call on you to chase away these ruthless invaders, who are laying it waste. Unless you rise in the majesty of your might, and exterminate their whole race, you may bid adieu to the hunting ground of your fathers, to the delicious flesh of the animals with which they once abounded, and to the skin with which you were once enabled to purchase your clothing and your rum."

By the time the Indians had crossed the Ohio, their numbers had reportedly grown to as many as 700 or 800. However, according to a British leader, Captain William Caldwell, his force consisted of only around three hundred men. Over a period of several days, the large army made its way, undetected, toward Bryan Station near Lexington. The strategy, to which Simon probably contributed, involved drawing parties of warriors from the main body and sending them to raid other stations and forts. This meant diverting militia from defense of Bryan Station — the real target of the expedition.

Upon reaching Bryan Station, the Indian army tried to conceal itself in an effort to gain the advantage of surprise. The occupants of Bryan Station became aware that there was a large army of Indians outside their gates, but they went about their activities as though they did not know the army was there. The defenders recognized the size and superiority of the Indian army. In an attempt to hopefully secure reenforcements for the 44 men defending the station, two men were dispatched to Lexington, Thomas Ball and Nicholas Thompson, to spread the word of the impending siege.

In the course of preparing for the assault, Bryan Station discovered that it was dangerously short of water. That shortage was very serious to the survival of the station, and it had the potential to make its defense difficult, if not impossible. The women of the fort bravely took their vessels and coolly opened the fort gates in the face of scores of pointed Indian rifles. Then they proceeded to make their normal journey to the station's water source. Once they reached the water source, they filled their containers and returned to the fort, unharmed, amid the silent cheers of their waiting families and friends. The Indians apparently preferred to let the women pass rather than reveal their presence and lose their supposed advantage of surprise.

The messengers that had been sent out earlier found that a large number of men were pursuing the Indians who had been sent to attack other forts and stations; therefore, they were not immediately available to come to the defense of Bryan Station. This also meant that the British diversionary plan had apparently worked. However, they were able to recruit 182 men who eventually gathered at Bryan Station. At that point, though, they found that the Indians had already abandoned the siege and departed, seeing as they weren't going to be able to take the fort without artillery with which to bring it down.

Having gathered the 182 men from Boonesborough, Lexington, Harrodsburg, and Boone Station, the officers set about planning their next move. They knew that Benjamin Logan was on his way north with a large force of men, and that he could provide sufficient reenforcements to assure the safety of the local militia and guarantee the success of any operation. Colonel John Todd of the Lexington settlement, who had served with George Rogers Clark in the Illinois campaign and who had attained a rank of lieutenant colonel, was the leading officer for any expeditions against the Indian Army. Stephen Trigg headed the militia of Lincoln County, and his assistant was Major Hugh McGary, a troublemaker who had a temper.

John and Stephen empanelled the other officers who would be in charge, including Daniel Boone for advice as to whether to pursue the Indian Army or wait until the Logan force arrived with its reenforcements. At the conference, tempers flared with Hugh when it was suggested that they wait for Benjamin and his men. John disagreed, arguing that they could hardly afford to let the Indians get away. He also scolded Hugh for his "timidity." The decision was made to pursue the Indians in the morning.

When John made his fateful decision, he had no inkling of the size of the Indian Army, which was apparently as many as 500 Indians, according to Daniel's estimates. He had no reconnaissance with which to estimate the size of the opposing force, its location, or its movements, and it appears that he was ill equipped to select a strategy that would best control the engagement.

He had only the advice and opinion of Daniel, who had very accurately predicted how many Indians were involved on behalf of the British based on the tracks laid down by the army and count of the campfires. He had hunted and explored the Blue Licks area and knew what lay ahead. He even predicted that the force was waiting in ambush, and that any attack might result in disaster. Smarting from the accusation that he was timid, Hugh needed a show of bravado in order to prove his courage. Unfortunately, Daniel's advice fell victim to Hugh's pride and temper.

As the American force pursued the Indians toward the Blue Licks, there was much sign of the Indians' past movements. However, there was no sign of their presence. Later, it was learned that the Indians were in possession of the high ground; they safely concealed themselves in ravines and behind trees and rocks.

The Indians' commander, Simon Girty, and others of the British hirelings must have been delighted to look down from their high positions and see the 182 Americans assembled on the opposite banks of the Licking River. To them, the Americans were easy targets, unaware of their vulnerability. They might have even seen the leaders of those men arguing with each other over whether to mount an assault, improve their position, or wait for Benjamin Logan's arrival with his armed troops.

Daniel made it clear at every opportunity that the Americans faced a large army of defenders and ambush. He pointed out the disadvantages of attacking the Indians head on and suggested that they wait for Benjamin, or at least realign their forces so as to attack the Indians at separate points, engulfing them in a pincer movement. What happened next is sometimes disputed, particularly the controversial actions of Hugh McGary. There are those who contend that Hugh's culpability was invented long after the battle, pointing to the fact that the incident is not mentioned in any of the reports, or by Daniel himself.

Suddenly, Hugh was in no mood to wait for Benjamin or to delay moving against the Indians. Already impatient with the discussion, he shouted, "By Godly, why not fight them then?" With that, he turned to Daniel and told him that he had never known him to be a coward.

Daniel struck back and replied, "No man has ever dared to call me a coward."

The argument reached a point of heightened anger, and Hugh yelled, "Them that ain't cowards follow me, and I'll show you where the yellow dogs are!" Hugh's men then fell in behind him and into the Licking River, leaving the other officers no choice but to join the attack.

The next five minutes were the worst Daniel had ever experienced. What has been described as an unplanned and undisciplined attack quickly fell into disarray, and the Americans began to fall all around him under the fire of hundreds of Indian rifles. After having reached the other bank and spurring his horse forward, Hugh quickly began a retreat and, passing Daniel, asked him why he was

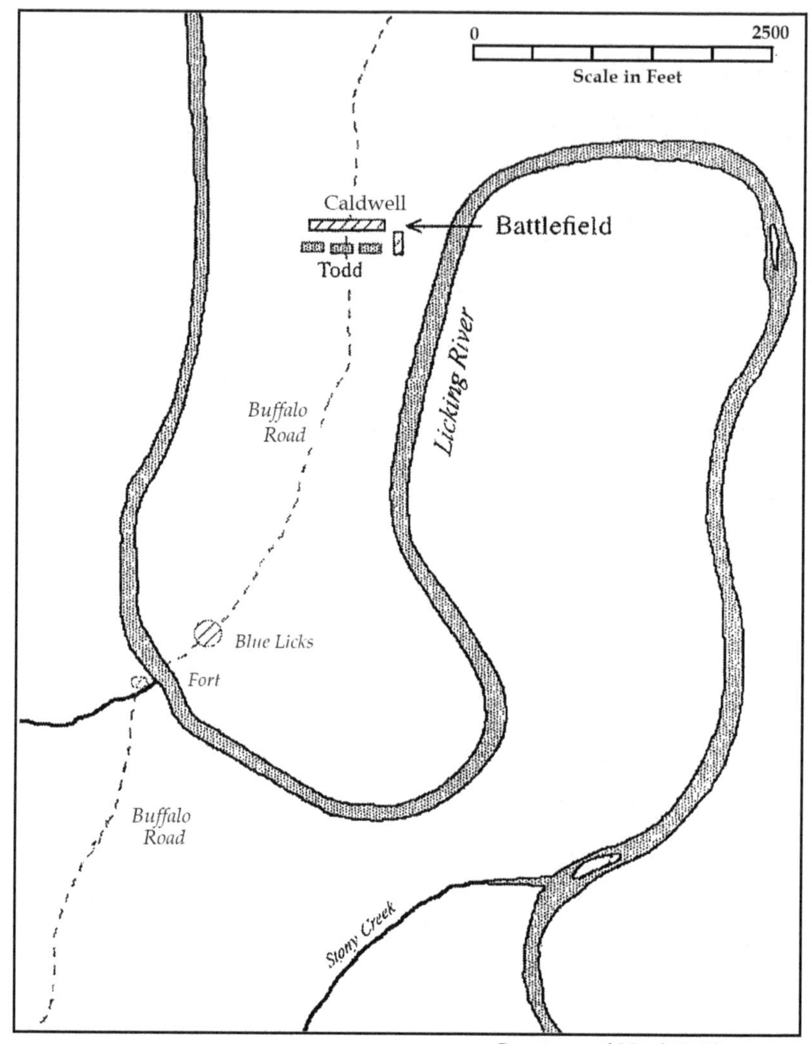

Courtesy of Neal O. Hammon

not also retreating.

Both John and Stephen were apparently killed from the first round of fire, as was Major Harlan. After witnessing the death of his second son, Israel, Daniel finally joined in the retreat. The Americans fled back across the river under a hail of bullets, with many giving up their blood to the Licking River and to the bank on the other side. Seventy-five Americans died in the battle. Daniel quickly returned to Boonesborough, giving Rebecca the sad news that Israel had been killed. That was the last battle fought in Henry Hamilton and De Peyster's war against the innocent Kentucky settlers who suffered from the outrages of that failed strategy.

News of the signing of an Armistice Treaty on April 19, 1783, ending the War of Separation from Great Britain brought great excitement to the frontier settlements of Kentucky. The settlers would soon begin to feel the salutary effects of the treaty on them, bringing increased safety from the marauding Indians as the greater benefit. The British stopped encouraging Indians to mount assaults on frontier settlements and ended its five-year bounty on American scalps.

Henry Hamilton's strategy of diversion proved to be a near failure. There were relatively few transfers of military assets from the colonies to the western frontier, and Tory sympathizers, who had fled the taunts of the eastern rebels, were as much the victims of the Hamilton strategy as were the others.

After his return from Kentucky in 1779, Daniel suffered another case of bad luck. It turned out that the improvements he had made to Boone Station were made for someone else's benefit; the land upon which it was built belonged to someone else. Probably anticipating an upheaval, he decided to cut his losses and move to a farm near Marble Creek approximately six miles away.

16
The Little Book

"My footsteps have often been marked with blood, and therefore I can truly subscribe to its original name. Two darling sons, and a brother, have I lost by savage hands, which have also taken from me forty valuable horses, and abundance of cattle. Many dark and sleepless nights have I been a companion for owls, separated from the cheerful society of men, scorched by the Summer's sun, and pinched by the Winter's cold, an instrument ordained to settle the wilderness. But now the scene is changed: Peace crowns the sylvan shade." —Colonel Daniel Boone

It was 1784, and 50 year old Daniel Boone and his family were living at Limestone, a town and riverboat harbor on the Ohio River between St. Louis and Pittsburgh near present-day Maysville. Daniel, along with approximately 20 other families, had moved from Boonesborough to Boone Station; then to Marble Creek; and finally to Limestone. Months had passed since Blue Lick.

Limestone had been popular for some time as a river destination for migrants who wanted to immigrate to Kentucky from regions north and east of that river, and who had decided to use it to make the long journey from Pittsburgh to the Kentucky wilderness. It was an ideal place to interrupt the hoards of newcomers migrating to Kentucky and who would need provisions necessary to survive in the wilderness.

Kentucky had really begun to grow in the years before 1785. In only a few short years, the population had soared from what had originally been just a few hearty hunters and adventurers scattered throughout the wilderness. By the time the Revolutionary War had ended, the spirit of enterprise and competition was being felt throughout the new republic. The colonists had long felt a land squeeze, and the available land was insufficient to meet the demands for expansion.

At the end of the war, thousands of acres of virgin land had become available to excited settlers and veterans of the war through a loose system of patents, grants, and purchases almost for the asking. Speculators were acquiring large tracts of land, sometimes for pennies an acre, and the best land was fast disappearing.

After 15 years in and out of the Kentucky wilderness, Daniel had realized that it was time for him to join the rest of the world. He was now over 50 years old. He had spent many of those years in solitude apart from his family. Wasn't it time to lay aside his rifle and moccasins, douse his campfire, and point his life in a different direction? He wanted to take advantage of the opportunities presented by the hoards of newcomers stopping at Limestone Harbor.

His old friend, Simon Kenton, had already made the move and even established the town of Washington nearby. Ever since his return to Kentucky in 1779, Daniel had considered such a change from his work as a woodsman and sometimes Indian fighter. He and others including his sons in law, Will Hayes and Flanders Callaway, had spent several days at the mouth of Limestone Creek on the Ohio River. They had probably even considered moving at that time.

Daniel's knowledge of Kentucky and his reputation as an adventurer would serve him well with the growing flood of newcomers. After all, had he not been one of the first to breach mountain barriers while fighting the hostile Indians? Had he not been first to build a fort on hostile ground? Had he not been first to settle his family behind pickets, exposing them to danger from Indian attacks? He had blazed the trail from Cumberland Gap to Central

Kentucky, enabling migrants to enter Kentucky from the south. He was now finally ready to quit a way of life that had taken so much from him and provided him with so little. The sacrifices he had made to the wilderness could not be measured. He had only recently led a group of militia in the Battle of Blue Lick where he lost his second son, Israel, to the cruelties of savage Indians.

He had spent most of his life as a wanderer, and years exploring Kentucky and helping settlers find new homes at great danger to himself, his family, and to those whom he had persuaded to join him. He had earlier lost another son in the Powell Valley. James, his oldest, had been brutally tortured, killed, and burned by yet another savage Indian. Additionally, Daniel had lost a brother to the same fate.

He had spent much time defending and safeguarding other new arrivals in scattered forts and stations throughout Kentucky. He took pride in the recognition that he had received from the new settlers, and he valued greatly the military commissions he had earned as an officer in the militia.

Things were beginning to change in the affairs of Kentucky. The dangers to migrants in their attempts to settle the new land had been reduced by developments on the military front, which were beginning to sequester the Shawnees and other tribes to the North of the Ohio River. General George Rogers Clark and others had taken care of much of the Indian problem by incursions into Ohio. Many hostile Indians, who had resisted white settlement, had fled to the north. A reduction of Indian raids against Kentucky settlers made work and movement much easier.

Many of the newcomers had probably already heard of the living legend, Daniel Boone, and the stories that were circulating about his exploits. They probably heard how he picked a fight with a bear, brought it to the ground, and then later had it for supper. Perhaps, they learned about how he bravely rescued his daughter and two other children from the clutches of Indian kidnappers.

Daniel had made his move to Limestone in 1784 after building a crude cabin and other structures made from keels of flatboats that had been dismantled and were no longer useable for river travel. John Mack Faragher described Limestone and the Boone property as follows:

"During the time the Boones lived there, from 1783 to 1789, Limestone consisted of no more than a dozen permanent households, ramshackle buildings, and wharves strung along the river. Boone owned a small warehouse and wharf for the loading and unloading of boats and the storage of goods, located a few hundred yards down-river from the mouth of Limestone Creek. Nearby was the Boone Tavern, what Nathan Boone called a 'house of entertainment.'"

He also described Daniel's early business conducted with his sons at Limestone:

"Boone did a brisk business in the lively market of Limestone. He fed travelers at Rebecca's table and provided sleeping facilities in the back room of the tavern. He supplied arriving emigrants with corn, flour, salt, beef, pork, dry goods, and housewares. He purchased country produce, skins or furs, ginseng root dug in the woods, corn whiskey distilled in backyard stills, collected it in his warehouse, and shipped it upriver to Pittsburgh on barges. His was mostly a barter business. In a typical receipt for goods Boone promised to pay a debt of f26.2.6 in 'Beaf or Pork, at the market price of this town,' and he used scrip, issued by a Louisville trader, backed by 'beaver skins.' His most valuable commodities were the horses raised on the rich limestone soils of the Bluegrass; much of his trading was aimed at the accumulation of herds that he sold in markets over the mountains."

From the beginning, many confused immigrants came into the store asking questions about Kentucky: Is it as good a place as they say? Where can we find a surveyor? Where can we get help staking a claim? Before long, Daniel had a book of accounts. He put together a surveying crew and began building a land business. He was even gathering ginseng to sell to the Chinese market. He was on a roll and it felt good.

Let's pause briefly to meet John Filson, the strange young man whose 'little book' brought Daniel Boone to the attention of the world, lifting him from obscurity to international fame. Shortly before Daniel moved to Limestone, a seismic event occurred in his life—one that assured the humble and unknown woodsman a place in history.

In 1784, John Filson, a newcomer to Kentucky, published 1,500 copies of a book, earning him the title of "Kentucky's first historian." The book sold for $1.25 a copy, and it included a new map of Kentucky. It had an appendix, containing a narrative of Daniel Boone's life on the frontier, and was read by millions of adventure seeking people over time. It was first published in North America and

England and soon translated into French and German.

John Filson was an ordinary looking man, approximately 30 years old, and a native of Chester County, Pennsylvania. He had a small inheritance from his father, which he used to buy land in Kentucky on the cheap. It is not known when he first came to Kentucky, but an early history of Lexington puts him there as a schoolteacher in 1782. John had decided to go west to view the property he had bought and seek his fortune as others were doing. Leaving for Kentucky by way of Pittsburgh, he took a barge down the Ohio River, very likely landing at Limestone.

In 1782, there was no reliable map of the region, and it was John's plan to create a map that could be used by the hoards of people coming to Kentucky in search of the so-called Golden Fleece. He probably intended to use the book to attract investors to his recently acquired property. At the time the book was being written, Daniel was likely living on the Marble Creek Farm. He had not yet moved to Limestone. We do not know when Daniel and John had crossed paths, but Daniel must have helped on the map that John was preparing either at Boone Station or Marble Creek.

John seemed out of place in the Kentucky wilderness. He has been portrayed as clumsy and inept, and he quickly became a nuisance because of his persistence in obtaining information for his book. When finally published, the book was entitled, *The Discovery, Settlement, and Present State of Kentucke*. It was described as containing an "essay toward the topography and natural history of that important country."

As mentioned, there was an appendix in the book including a narrative, entitled, *The Adventures of Colonel Daniel Boon*. [sic] Also included in the appendix was the new map of Kentucky "drawn from actual surveys." The map turned out to be useful, depicting much of the known landscape, rivers, streams, and other topography, and including the location of several forts, settlements, and stations.

The Adventures of Colonel Daniel Boon has endured years of scrutiny by many scholars. It tells a story about the life of Daniel Boone, his philosophy, a description of the Kentucky wilderness, and a narrative of his experiences as a woodsman in that wilderness. Many critics have concluded from the stilted language used and the philosophical ramblings that John penned it, not Daniel.

Soon after it was published in North America, England, France, and Germany in 1784, the narrative relating the adventures of Daniel Boone started to gain recognition. We need not list the honors paid to him as a result of that book. Counties and national parks have been named after him. Scores of books have been written about his life by authors who have scoured the archives for information to include in their writings; he even had a long running television series named after him. Additionally, he was noticed by classical writers such as Waldo Emerson and Lord Byron. Daniel Boone became a folk hero, not only in America, but also in much of the world, for his reputation as a man of nature.

Daniel's contributions to the settlement of Kentucky are substantial; however, so are those of James Harrod, Simon Kenton, and hundreds of other adventurers who stood their ground against the same perils with as much dignity and resolve, but didn't have their adventures romanticized by the imaginative John Filson.

We also learned that this man of reputed compassion had even acquired several slaves. Rebecca kept busy, managing the kitchen, which was probably easy work after years of raising little gardens, sometimes on rocky hillsides, and watching out for a truant husband, who always seemed to be on a horse, bound for a two year hunt or a fort or station under siege.

At the end of Daniel's biography, more than 16 years before he moved to Missouri, he told Filson about his love for Kentucky and his hopes for its future:

> "I now live in peace and safety, enjoying the sweets of liberty, and the bounties of Providence, with my once fellow-sufferers, in this delightful country, which I have seen purchased with a vast [expanse] of blood and treasure, delighting in the prospect of its being, in a short time, one of the most opulent and powerful states on the continent of North America; which with the love and gratitude of my countrymen, I esteem a sufficient reward for all my toil and dangers."

Daniel, both before and after his move to Limestone, had made numerous claims to thousands of acres of public lands over the years, but many of his land titles had not been perfected and were lost to persons making adverse claims of ownership to the property. His surveys of his own property were often inaccurate, and someone else would claim the property, leading to lawsuits against him to quiet title. He ignored many of those lawsuits, letting the property go by default.

In the brief time since Blue Licks, Daniel accumulated substantial debts for loans and for credit. Those debts, together with a failed land deal with the infamous Imlay, were growing larger as the months went by. Disappointed clients who had hired him to survey or buy property were beginning to sue him for damages, claiming that invalid surveys or other problems with their titles had caused them to lose their property.

Daniel spent much of his time appearing in courts as a witness, testifying for clients who had been sued, and who needed to support their lawsuits with testimonies from him. Although it is not known just how many lawsuits Daniel had against him, he was clearly overwhelmed to the point where he needed a lawyer to defend himself. After five long years, Daniel grew weary of the constant conflicts and accusations of fraud and wrongdoing, and he had apparently taken all he could take. He decided to walk away and leave his business in the hands of his children.

In 1789, Daniel moved once again, this time to Point Pleasant at the mouth of the Kanawha River in West Virginia. After resigning his official offices — including his military commission, his position as coroner, and his position as state representative — and turning over the Limestone businesses to his son-in-law, Will Hayes, he was finally free of the myriad troubles he had been facing.

With that, Daniel decided to begin the operation of a small store at Point Pleasant. At the store, he traded skins, furs, and other commodities. Despite his financial problems, and while he had managed to escape the frowns and sneers of debt collectors and process servers, his reputation as a woodsman and adventurer continued to grow both in America and abroad.

Daniel got involved in civic pursuits and was elected to the Virginia Legislature. Then he did some surveying and was eventually appointed lieutenant colonel, heading the militia. He even resumed his favorite activity: roaming the countryside in search of game.

In 1794, the Boone family returned to Brushy Fork, Kentucky, near Blue Licks, and moved into a cabin that Daniel built on property owned by his son, Daniel. The family lived there for approximately four years, reputedly under difficult circumstances with little or no income, while living largely on a diet of game, berries, greens, and garden crops.

Not everyone agrees that Daniel was poor, contending that he had income from land sales and hunt-ing. Daniel was, however, able to get surveying jobs, which were still to be had in abundance. Additionally, there was always sap to be taken from the maple trees that he could turn into maple syrup and sell. To this day, the Brushy Fork cabin that Daniel built still stands and may be seen near the Blue Licks State Park between Paris, Kentucky, and Maysville where the lines of the Battle of Blue Licks are drawn and may be studied.

17
Boone in Exile

"The small Spanish garrison paraded, with flags unfurled, drums rolling, sabers flashing in an impressive display. It would be the only time in his life that Boone received military honors." —John Mack Faragher, The Life and Legend of an American Pioneer

Daniel Morgan Boone, Daniel's son, was hunting on the Mississippi River in 1795 when he decided to investigate reports he had heard of rich lands in Spanish owned Missouri to the west of Kentucky. On that trip, he met Spanish Lieutenant Governor Don Zenon Trudeau, who very cordially received him and who frankly advised him that Spain needed new settlers to occupy its rich domains in Missouri and would welcome the famed Daniel Boone, who had so distinguished himself.

Young Daniel went back to Missouri in 1798 with a firm resolve to claim some of the available land. In 1799, he returned to Kentucky where he conferred with his father, giving him glowing reports about the fertile Missouri landscape and other aspects of the available property. Based on the young Boone's reconnaissance, Daniel, the patriarch of the Boone family, made the decision that he, Rebecca, and all of his family and extended family would accompany his son to the new land, leaving Kentucky forever.

Life in Kentucky had become so odious for the elder Daniel, and his financial condition had become so dire that he knew he had to flee the debt collectors and grouchers, even if it meant giving up the remaining land that he had won in the years he spent exploring and settling Kentucky.

Before he agreed to move to Missouri, however, the Spanish Lieutenant Governor Trudeau promised him a large tract of land and additional property for any new settlers that he might bring to Missouri. Also, he was given the right to select the property that would be granted to him as well as the property to be granted to those who accompanied him.

Under the agreement, Daniel was to receive 1,000 arpents, or acres, and the settlers would receive 400 arpents, plus additional acreage for chosen and other designated members of the settlement. It was later proposed by the Spanish that Daniel attract an additional 100 new settlers to Missouri, which would increase his grants to 10,000 arpents.

Under Missouri law, all such grants were conditioned upon the grantee occupying the property and making certain improvements, including certain structures and clearing ten acres annually until ten percent of the property had been cleared. Carlos De Lassus, however, advised Daniel that the occupancy requirements did not apply to officials of the government; he would be excused from that requirement. But that assurance was not given in writing and nothing was filed with the government in New Orleans.

In preparation for the move to Missouri, Daniel hollowed out a large canoe that measured 60 feet long. It would could carry several tons of Daniel's plunder as well as some members of the Boone family. By the time they all began the journey, Daniel had achieved some considerable prominence. The move was highly publicized and drew attention to the new settlements to the west of the Mississippi, which were owned by the Spaniards. While Daniel and some others, including a couple of black slaves, drove the cattle, horses, pigs, and other stock across the sometimes rough terrain, fording rivers, and other obstacles, another party floated the large dugout canoe down the Mississippi River into Missouri.

On the way, they passed through Cincinnati,

where they met a crowd gathered to see and meet the famed Daniel Boone. It was no secret that he was leaving Kentucky. When a bystander asked why he was leaving, Daniel replied, "Too many people. Too crowded! I want more elbow room."

The trip to Missouri was, in some ways, like the move from Exeter to the Yadkin Valley; but, Daniel was 50 years older and much smarter now. He had traveled thousands of miles by foot across Indian warriors' paths on his way to places where no white man had ever been.

But, there he was again, on his way to a place he had never seen, to dwell among people he did not know. He could only hope that the game was as abundant as he found it in the wilderness in the Yadkin Valley, and the memories as enduring. He was leaving everything behind to start all over again. However, he was not afraid. All along the route of travel, well wishers showed up to see the great Daniel Boone in person.

It was not until October that the entourage reached St. Louis, Missouri, with a celebration honoring the new citizen, Daniel Boone, and his family. Spanish Lieutenant Governor Trudeau and his successor were delighted with the progress that the new immigrants had made and treated them with dignity and respect:

"American and Spanish flags were displayed. The garrison paraded, and Lieutenant Colonel Boone, late of the Kanawha County Militia, was received with the honors due his rank. It was probably the first time in his life that the tough old fighter had ever seen the frills and furbelows of army life. The militia in Kaintuck' simply went out, killed its Indians, and hurried home to its families, troubling its heads very little over military pomp and pageantry, thankful enough to have them still unscalped.

"When the official formalities were over, the simples [sic] old man in the leather hunting shirt with a couple of knives in the belt mounted his 'sad looking horse', took his rifle, whistled to the three or four hunting dogs that accompanied him, and set out for the home of his son Daniel Morgan Boone, sixty miles farther on."

In 1798, the Kentucky General Assembly voted to name a recently formed county in honor of Daniel Boone. That was one of the pleasantries he could point to with pride. The irony is that, in the same year, the sheriffs of Mason and Clark Counties advertised and sold more than 10,000 acres of his land for nonpayment of taxes. Daniel thought that was a contradiction, but he probably brushed it off with his customary shrug.

So how did Daniel Boone, now 65, spend his first day and night in exile? He was dejected but hopeful, penniless but on his way back. He was plodding his way through 60 miles of near-wilderness much like the landscape in Kentucky.

He had learned to adapt to such consequences of adventure so long as there was bountiful game nearby. His immediate concern was probably whether the beaver would rut on schedule and where he would find help to pick the best place to set his traps. He hoped the game was as plentiful as the Spaniards said. He looked forward to being able to set up a good long hunt with his sons, maybe over in Kansas, or even farther away.

He finally reached the cabin of his son, Daniel, tired from the long trip from Kentucky. But he probably wasn't too tired to spend some time exploring the new venue to plan his first hunt in Missouri after a good night's sleep. If anyone had thought that Daniel had moved to Missouri to retire, they were wrong.

He had found land with an abundance of game that he hunted with great pleasure just as his son had described it. He looked forward to hunting with companions or members of the family in places that had only been lightly hunted. He was pleased to find the hunting in Missouri not unlike the hunting in Kentucky. Almost as soon as he reached Missouri, Daniel began trapping the rivers and streams, and he continued even past his eightieth birthday to the consternation of his family and friends.

The prices paid by the St. Charles traders for furs and skins were so inadequate that he began taking them to St. Louis, a 60 mile journey. At times, it seemed like rheumatism or some other problem might keep Daniel from continuing his hunting and trapping, but he nearly always recuperated in time to go along as planned. During his latter years, the freezing temperatures or physical stress upon his aging body kept him from joining his son, Daniel, or some of his other companions, and he would sadly agree to stay at home.

On July 11, 1800, Carlos De Lassus, the new Lieutenant Governor, appointed Boone as Syndic for the Femme Osage. That appointment placed him in complete charge of the civil and military affairs of the entire area. In his new post, the humble Daniel designated himself as "Commander of the District of Femme Osage." In this new position, Daniel became quite powerful. He witnessed notes, punished crimes, kept order, settled estates, assigned vacant lands, and performed many other functions. He must have made an interesting figure as a justice of the peace.

He usually administered justice under a tree close to his cabin, which he called the "Justice Tree." Dressed as a woodsman, he wrote his own laws and fashioned his own judgments on a case-by-case basis, according to procedures that were of his own making. There appeared to be little or no complaint on the part of litigants. [They really had no right of appeal even if they were aggrieved by his actions.]

Daniel had much work to be done, parceling out land to the many Boone émigrés. Trudeau wanted to be sure that his word would be kept by any successor, and he entrusted Daniel with blank grants that he was authorized to use in distributing and locating property to the his settlers. Daniel's effort to settle the area for Missouri proved to be very successful, and the Spanish officials were only too glad to give him responsibility for distributing that property to the new émigrés.

Things in Missouri went well until the United States bought the Missouri territory through the Louisiana Purchase. When Missouri became a territory of the United States in late 1803, the American government promised that the legitimate claims of the immigrants would be honored under a smooth transfer of power.

But, it soon appeared that Daniel's claim to his property might not stand because he, again, had failed to perfect his titles to properties in the manner required by the Spanish government. After several years of delay, a decision finally made by the newly formed United States Land Commission determined that Daniel's grant was subject to the occupancy requirements in effect under Spanish law, and that his failure to comply with the Spanish law rendered his grant invalid.

Daniel's counsel, a man of considerable influence with the United States Congress and who apparently was an adroit lawyer, petitioned the United States Congress for a 10,000 acre grant for Daniel's years of public service to Kentucky and to the United States. The petition wound its way through the legislative process, resulting in a recommendation that the petition be granted.

But again, Boone's bad luck dealt him a blow. One of the Missouri territory delegates to Congress made an offhand remark that all Daniel wanted was the original grant of 1,000 arpents. So, Daniel's donation grant from the United States was limited to 1,000 arpents which he, at first, was going to refuse. However, during a Congressional recess, he agreed to accept it after consultation with his family and representatives. Daniel Boone had fought—and won—his last battle. The prize, as could be expected, was land.

Rebecca died at Jemima's house in 1813. Daniel lived another seven years in reasonably good health among his family and friends. Then, at the age of 86, the old hunter passed away.

Requiem:

"Under the wide and starry sky

Dig the grave and let me lie:

Glad did I live and gladly die,

And I laid me down with a will.

This be the verse you grave for me:

Here he lies where he long'd to be;

Home is the sailor, home from the sea,

And the hunter home from the hill."

—Robert Louis Stevenson

Epilogue

The exploits of Daniel Boone and much of what he has said have been popularized and romanticized in a plethora of biographies, ten cent novels, comic books, essays, poems, magazines, outdoor dramas, commercials, and other sources. Daniel was even the subject of a six year national television series (165 episodes total) that was filled with legend, myth, and hype —most of it coming straight from the imagination of the show's script writers.

The old hunter in life became the hunted in death. Portrait painters traveled to his home in Missouri to work their magic and pass his likeness on to other generations of adventurers. Aspiring authors combed the back roads and archives, looking for one more fragment of Daniel Boone history to be passed on to avid readers. Private collectors and museums vied for artifacts—things that were later found to be of little or no historic value. Daniel was even portrayed as a kind of mystical symbol, representing the inevitability of American growth and expansion. To some folks, he became a personification of the "natural man," the gay philosopher, and one writer's rootin' tootin' Indian killer. The humble old man, even before he died, must have sensed the coming makeover. He complained:

"Many heroic actions and chivalrous adventures are related of me, which exist only in the regions of fantasy. With me, the world has taken great liberties, and yet, I have been but a common man.

"Are you looking for the real Daniel Boone? You'd never find him in a corn patch or digging turnips out of poor yellow dirt. He hated garden work and avoided it whenever he could. Perhaps, you could find him sangin' for ginseng or helping Rebecca tap one of the huge maple trees for syrup. You definitely wouldn't find him in the St. Louis, Missouri, lyceum, listening to Friday's lecture on Manifest Destiny, or lamenting the demise of 'the natural man.'

"You might find him in the Powell Valley, searching out the illusive Cumberland Gap, or trudging across the Kentucky wilderness on his way to explore the Falls of the Ohio. He might be wintering in a cave with Benjamin Cutbirth on Hickman Creek, wrapped in a buffalo robe and running their traps from time to time. Then again, he could be blazing a road through Cumberland Gap to Boonesborough. With all of that said, however, you'll most likely find him and his old companions from the Yadkin Valley on a long hunt through the wilds of Kentucky. That was Daniel Boone's true passion.

"'Here, boys, let's stop right here,' he might say, looking down Station Camp Creek. 'Here's where we'll set up the base camp. It's got plenty of water close by, and I think I remember a little salt spring about a mile on down the way. It's got a canebrake in case the Shawnees pay us a visit, too. Cooley, you and Cutbirth stay here and build a station camp and shelters. While you're doing that, Finley, you can look around for some dry firewood and start us a fire close to sundown. Neely, you and Holden can start chopping uprights from that little grove of poplars over there for the shelters. I'll take a little run and see what I can find by way of game. We'll try to be back by sundown with a turkey or two to roast. Tomorrow, me and Stewart'll hunt that ridge over there to the north. You all can pick out where you want to hunt. But, if it was me, I'd take the hollow to the right and hunt it to the top of the ridge.' The old hunter would then mount his little Indian pony, shoulder his rifle, and ride off into that vast Kentucky wilderness. He'd probably grin to himself, feeling good to have his old buddy, John Stewart, on a long hunt with him again.

"No, Daniel Boone won't be hard to find if you just look in the right spot. He's back in Kentucky again, approximately 155 miles north of Cumberland Gap near Frankfort, recruiting his horses and his companions, readying for the next big hunt. But, if you're going to go look for him, you better watch out for Dragging Canoe and his band of warring Cherokees. They may be in a bad mood.

"Thus we behold Kentucky, lately a howling wilderness, the habitation of savages and wild beasts, become a fruitful field; this region, so favorably distinguished by na-

ture, now become the habitation of civilization." — Colonel Daniel Boone

Bibliography

Bakeless, John; *Daniel Boone: Master of the Wilderness*, New York, William Morrow, 1939.

Belue, Ted Franklin; *The Long Hunt: Death of the Buffalo East of the Mississippi*. Stackpole, 1996.

Butterfield, Consul Willshire; *History of the Girtys*, Reprinted, Log Cabin Shop, Inc. 1995.

Clark, Thomas D.; *A History of Kentucky*, New York: Prentice-Hall, 1937

Collins, Lewis; *Historical Sketches of Kentucky*. Cincinnati, Ohio, Collins & James, 1847.

Draper, Lyman Copeland; *The Life of Daniel Boone*. Edited by Ted Franklin Belue. Mechanicsburg, Penn., Stackpole, 1998.

Faragher, John Mack; *Daniel Boone: The Life and Legend of an American Pioneer*, New York: Holt, 1992.

Filson, John; *The Discovery, Settlement and Present State of Kentucke*, 1784, Reprint, New York: Corinth Books, 1962.

George Rogers Clark Papers, Illinois Historical Collections, Page xxxvi.

Germain to Carlton, March 26, 1777, Michigan Pioneer Collections, Vol. IX, pp. 346, 347.

Hammon, Neal O.; *My Father, Daniel Boone*, The University Press of Kentucky, 1999

Hammon, Neal, and Richard Taylor; *Virginia's Western War, 1775-1786*, Mechanicsburg, Penn, Stackpole Books, 2002.

Lofaro, Michael A. Daniel Boone; *An American Life*. Lexington: University Press of Kentucky, 2003.

About the Author

Eugene Goss is a retired lawyer who practiced in Harlan County, Kentucky for over fifty years. He undertook this book about Daniel Boone and Kentucky soon after retirement.

After the first edition of *The Wanderer: Daniel Boone's Kentucke*, he authored two novels: *Atlanta Rain* and *Summerville*.

Index

BOONE, Daniel

The End

□

CPSIA information can be obtained
at www.ICGtesting.com
Printed in the USA
LVHW011746300620
659399LV00015B/1458